Explorations in
Crime and Justice

Explorations in Crime and Justice: A Casebook

JAMES L. MASSEY
Northern Illinois University

SUSETTE M. TALARICO
University of Georgia

ALLYN AND BACON

Boston   London   Sydney   Toronto

Series Editor: Karen Hanson
Series Editorial Assistant: Susan S. Brody
Editorial-Production Service: York Production Services
Cover Administrator: Linda K. Dickinson
Manufacturing Buyer: Bill Alberti

Library of Congress Cataloging-in-Publication Data

Massey, James Lewis.
    Explorations in crime and justice: a casebook / James L. Massey,
Susette M. Talarico.
      p. cm.
    Includes bibliographical references.
    ISBN 0-205-12174-8
    1. Criminal justice, Administration of--Case studies. 2. Criminal
justice, Administration of--United States--Case studies.
    I. Talarico, Susette M.   II. Title.
HV7419.M37 1990
364--dc20   89-38538
                                 CIP

Printed in the United States of America

10 9 8 7 6 5 4 3   94 93 92 91 90 89

To Dori, Karen, and June
         and
to the students and faculty of the University of Georgia
Criminal Studies Program

Contents

viii

Preface

The case method of instruction was developed and has been traditionally associated with the Harvard Business School. The teaching method, however, is used in business and public administration programs across the country and has recently been extended to other areas of study. In this text we offer an application to the study of criminal justice.

The centerpiece of the case method mode of learning is the individual "case" which has been defined by Megginson (1980, "The Case Method as Both a Research Technique and Pedagogic Method," *Case Research Journal,* pp. 10-18) as "a real-life situation researched and produced by scholars with such detailed, sufficient care and fidelity that it permits the inclusion of sufficient environmental facts of a situation involving real people and events, which occurred in a real organization." Simply put, an effective case, used in a discussion context, makes its greatest contribution to learning as an instrument designed to promote the decision-making and problem-solving skills of individual students. It is a particularly logical choice for organizing class discussion because it makes explicit assumptions about the role of the instructor, the student, and the instructional process in achieving specific learning objectives.

Much of the popularity of the case method in business schools is based on the recognition that managers are expected to develop and possess skills that will enable them to be effective in solving diverse organizational problems. A similar concern confronts faculty in virtually all academic specialties that contribute to the education of students whose performance in the workplace will be judged on competencies that pertain to, and are exercised within, complex organizations. But faculty must also respond to the fundamental social expectation that the beneficiaries of a college education have the capacity to think in a timely, logical, insightful, and critical fashion. Within management and business administration curricula, advocates of the case method have repeatedly demonstrated its capacity to contribute significantly to the fulfillment of this objective. We hope that our contribution will extend this to criminal justice as well.

The cases included in this text are oriented toward two educational objectives. The first of these is to provide students with the motivation to become active rather than passive learners. Discussion-based teaching is clearly one strategy of doing this. If discussion is to reach the second, higher order objective of converting situationally active learning into a *way* of learning, we must be prepared to provide the kind of support necessary to bring both objectives to fruition. This is where the case method achieves its optimal utility. It is a powerful device through which students can explore issues defined by the empirical world and, in the process, learn the advantages of a formal approach to solving real problems.

The cases that we offer for use in criminal justice courses are fictionalized accounts of real-life problems and situations in criminal justice or composites of several. The dialogue is invented with quotations merely indicative of speech and not actual utterances. Each case, however, is prepared so that students across the country can use the material in their courses and so that no privacy or confidentiality is violated. In this text are twenty original cases that focus on the three major components of the criminal justice system (law enforcement, courts, and corrections) and that deal with special topics in the study of crime and justice. The casebook, consequently, is divided into four major sections, each preceded by a short introduction that outlines the topics and concepts. Following each case is a set of discussion questions, although individual instructors and students may prefer to draft their own queries.

Explorations in Crime and Justice: A Casebook may be used as the primary text for an instructor who adopts the Harvard Business School model for his/her course. This can be attempted with small and large classes. In fact, the Harvard Business School model is most frequently applied in large sections. In addition to use as a primary text, *Explorations in Crime and Justice: A Casebook* could also serve as a supplement to the more traditional textbook. In this adoption, it would serve as a useful vehicle for discussion sections organized around large lecture classes, or as a guide to directed discussions with seminar or average-sized classes. However it is used, we hope that it will stimulate more active learning on the part of students and a rich appreciation of the complexity of the problems and issues that confront criminal justice practitioners and scholars in our society.

As indicated in the dedication, the authors are grateful to the staff, students, and faculty of the University of Georgia Criminal Justice Studies Program who inspired this project and who contribute to our continued enthusiasm for criminal justice education. We also appreciate initial support from the UGA Office of Instructional Development. In particular, we are grateful to Ronald Simpson, William Jackson, and Frank Gillespie for the instructional improvement grant that helped us to develop and test pilot cases. We would also like to thank Professor Marc Gertz of Florida State University, Professor Dennis Hoffman of University of Nebraska, Omaha, and Professor Christine Sellers of Northern Arizona University for their helpful reviewing of our manuscript. Finally, we acknowledge the seemingly inexhaustible support and encouragement provided by our spouses, Carrie and Rodger, and our children, Ted, Drew, and Robert.

PART ONE
Law Enforcement

Introduction

Law enforcement represents the first of three major criminal justice processes. Included in this segment of the criminal justice system are police departments and agencies at the local, state, and federal levels of government. As students of criminal justice know, police play a pivotal part in the administration of criminal law because their decisions and actions shape the work of those who labor in the judicial and correctional arenas.

Contemporary law enforcement is distinguished by some classical and current issues. These include the exercise of police discretion, the variety of demands confronting law enforcement agencies, the concern with civil liability, and the multifaceted professionalism characteristic of contemporary policing.

The exercise of discretionary authority is not a new issue in law enforcement, but it probably is one of its more intractable dimensions. Scholars and practitioners agree that discretionary authority is inevitable. However, they do not always agree on the most efficacious way to regulate the exercise of discretion or the appropriate means of censuring abuses of police power. Although each of the cases included in this section is related to this dimension of police work, *Mercy, Mercy, Lady* deals with the topic directly. This case explores the rather routine exercise of discretionary authority in traffic control with an additional reference to the use of deadly force. Although the two discretionary situations are not comparable, the reader is encouraged to look at the differences and parallels in the trivial and drastic exercise of police power.

There are a variety of demands that are placed on police officers and police departments. In his classic study of law enforcement in several communities, James Q. Wilson (1968, *Varieties of Police Behavior,* Cambridge, MA: Harvard University Press.) argued that three contrasting expectations are placed on police—demands for the enforcement of the law, for the maintenance of order, and for service. At different times in a given department and at different points in an individual officer's career, these three demands will be felt. Wilson, however, additionally observes that some departments are more characterized by a single demand over a long period of time. *What Do We Do With 2,000 Streakers?* looks at the demands placed on police in unusual or atypical circumstances. In this case, a campus police department is asked to maintain order when a large number of students elect to streak through campus. At the same time, the department's leaders and its line officers have to deal with some individual demands for law enforcement, demands that cannot be applied in a selective, much less full, capacity in the situation. As the reader learns about the two different demands and the vulnerable position of the police department, he/she also has to consider the limits of law enforcement and the sometimes tenuous relationship between the police and the community they serve.

Police and other people who exercise public authority are currently very concerned about civil liability. As part of the more general litigation crisis, this concern focuses on lawsuits that seem to have increased in recent years, lawsuits wherein citizens seek monetary damages for alleged abuses of police power. Although empirical evidence on the extent of litigation and the size of monetary damages is very limited, there is considerable attention to the effect that the civil liability crisis has had not only on the exercise of street-level discretion but also on the management of police departments. The case *But It Was an Accident* tells the story of a civil suit that was filed against an individual officer and his department. In this account, the reader confronts a specific case and has to consider the merits of the plaintiff's and the defendant's positions and the degree to which the department supported or betrayed the officer in question. In concluding this case, the reader is asked to consider the implications that civil litigation carries for police work and for the selection and supervision of police personnel.

Police professionalism is an issue that has dominated much of law enforcement for the past twenty years. Taking many guises, professionalism covers the training and education of officers, the salary scales for police work, the manner in which departments are organized and administered, and the variety of behavior that is or is not condoned. For professional law enforcement officers and administrators, police corruption is both an embarrassment and a serious affront to the law. Two cases, *Hard Time Finding Charlie* and *We've Got a Serious Problem Here,* explore different dimensions of this facet of police professionalism. In *Hard Time Finding Charlie* the reader confronts a police officer who has routinely succumbed to some ordinary forms of corruption. In the case, a younger, more professional officer has to deal with one who is older, and less professional. In the process, both experience considerable frustration with their contrasting expectations of what police work is about. Both offer substantial challenges to the department in question. *We've Got a Serious Problem Here* details the story of more serious police corruption, specifically police participation in criminal activity. In this case, we learn of a small town sheriff who is making a considerable amount of money in narcotics, a fact that puts him at variance with the norms of professional policing and the criminal law.

All five cases in this section deal with enduring issues in law enforcement. The following chart outlines the central concepts and issues so that the reader has an overview of the points illustrated and an outline of the discussion topics that these cases were designed to stimulate. In the process, it is the authors' hope that students will offer their own examples and additional stories that can be used to illuminate these classic issues in law enforcement.

PART ONE: Law Enforcement

Case Title	Central Subject	Concepts/Issues
Mercy, Mercy, Lady	police discretion	exercise of discretion selective law enforcement use of deadly force
What Do We Do With 2,000 Streakers'?	policing in unusual circumstances	order maintenance demands on police limits of police power police–community relations conceptions of criminal behavior relationship between law and morality
But it was an Accident	police liability	officer and departmental liability challenges to police actions liability crisis
Hard Time Finding Charlie	police professionalism and corruption	police corruption supervising in law enforcement professionalism policing in transition
We've Got a serious Problem Here	police corruption and drug traffic	police criminality entrapment professionalism

5

Case One

Mercy, Mercy, Lady

It was early one June morning and virtually no other driver was in sight on Interstate 85. The skies were clear, the temperature was already a warm 75 degrees. The early morning quiet—it was barely 5:00 a.m.—was broken only by the noise of the radio—some comfort and companionship as Sally Cribari drove north to visit her family and friends. Sally lived in the southeast and faced a drive of about a thousand miles to get home. Typically, she took these trips two or three times a year and just as typically started at 3:00 a.m. on a Sunday to avoid the heavy weekday traffic and, as she put it, "to make some time." Make time she did as she usually drove at least 600 miles the first day and rather regularly exceeded the posted speed limit.

This Sunday was no exception. Sally was driving at approximately 75 m.p.h. as she drove into a new state on the highway. The only indication that you were crossing jurisdictional lines was a sign posted at the state line which welcomed you to North Carolina. "Ah," Sally mused to herself, "North Carolina. At this rate, I should be in Maryland or even New Jersey by night time. I can easily hit Vermont Monday afternoon."

Sally's satisfaction and smugness, however, were abruptly broken when she noticed a siren in the distance. As her heartbeat accelerated, she looked in her rearview mirror and saw the blue light that only topped police cruisers. "Oh no," she said to no one in particular, "I'm going to get a ticket." Slowing down, Sally moved her bright red Honda to the side of the road and waited for the trooper to come over with the ticket.

As he approached the car, Trooper Wilson cried out in an excited but nonetheless pleasant drawl, "Mercy, mercy, lady. Where are you going?" "Would you believe Vermont," Sally replied honestly. "Well at the rate you're going, it won't take long," Wilson responded. "Didn't you see me back there?" he added. "Of course not," Sally observed. "If I saw you, I would have slowed down." Well," Wilson continued, "you sure didn't slow down. Do you know what I clocked you at?" "Have no idea," Sally said, "although I suspect it was somewhere in the neighborhood of 70 m.p.h." "75," Wilson responded.

The remainder of the conversation continued in a more relaxed way as Sally realized that Wilson, however likely to give a ticket, was pleasant and cordial. "Well," Wilson went on, "I know it's early and the roads are clear, but 75 is sure fast. Fifty-five's still the speed limit and I just can't let you go much beyond that." Sally didn't argue. She had long since learned that it was usually pointless to try to argue her way out of a ticket. Nor did she try to impress or cajole the officer into being easy. As she explained to a friend after, "I just can't pull the helpless female number. I like to drive fast but I'm a good driver. It's been years since I had an accident!"

Wilson was toying with letting Sally off—she didn't contest the speeding, she didn't offer some half-baked excuse, and she didn't try the pretty legs routine. But she was going 75! And, besides, things were pretty slow. Stalling for some time to make up his mind, Wilson asked Sally about her car, the make, and her general assessment of its handling. Finally, he looked at her and remarked, "I've got to give you a ticket. I mean I can't let you off the hook completely." Sally didn't argue. She knew as soon as the blue light appeared in the rearview mirror that it was pay-up time. "OK," Sally said, "I know you've got to do your job."

Wilson left Sally's car and returned to the cruiser to write the ticket. As Sally waited she began to think about the fine she'd have to pay and wondered what the North Carolina scale was. Wilson came back, handed her her ticket, license, and registration, and told her he was going to write her up for 65. "You'll still have to pay a fine," he observed, "but it won't be as much as if I wrote up your real speed. Let me give you a piece of advice, though," he continued. "Stick close to 65—a lot of troopers won't pull you over if you're slightly above the speed limit. But twenty miles beyond is just asking for trouble. So, stay close to 65 and drive carefully."

Sally took the ticket and noticed that her fine was $60. Well, I guess I'm lucky, she thought. It could have been worse. Sally took the trooper's advice and tried to stick close to the speed limit. When she did increase speed, she was careful to stay below 65 and paid particular attention to cars parked alongside the highway. As she continued her drive to Vermont, she listened to local radio stations. Sometime during the remainder of the drive, Sally picked up a national news report on a metropolitan radio station. Although Sally paid considerable attention to national and international news reports, she abruptly "took in" a more local report when the announcer summarized a police shooting that had occurred in Metro City.

With a center city of about three-quarters of a million and a metropolitan area of some four million people, Metro City was the proverbial "big town." Like many other cities of its size, Metro City had a substantial number of citizens living below the poverty line. Along with this were the standard public housing projects, many of which had been built years earlier and were now run down and, indeed, dangerous. The incident featured in the radio news report had taken place at one of these projects and the details were rather grim. Saturday evening, Metro police received a report that an armed man was threatening several people in one of the city's more congested and troublesome projects. Apparently, the call did not come in on the emergency 911 line—many project residents didn't like to use the 911 number because calls were immediately traced—so it took some time before the police dispatcher could identify the problem and location. When the Metro police car finally arrived, the armed man, one Reginald Talbert, was brandishing a gun and pointing it at several people. "Do something, man," yelled one of the observers who by that time were afraid to make a quick exit from the project yard. As the two officers, Bud Canale and Joe Rudder, moved in, they called to Talbert to drop his gun. Talbert waved the weapon and challenged the cops to come and get him. From his actions and manner, it appeared that Talbert had had too much to drink. Whatever the source of the problem, the gun was real and the folks nearby were clearly afraid. Quickly, the police moved in and wrestled Talbert to the ground. As Rudder started to put handcuffs on Talbert, the suspect reached for the gun that had dropped to the ground. Without a warning, Canale fired several shots leaving Talbert dead. The crowd that had originally called for the police's assistance quickly seemed to take Talbert's side. "You didn't have to do that," one man cried, while a middle-aged woman yelled an obscenity and cried "killers!"

The news report didn't provide any more information about the killing other than to note that the Metro Police Department had suspended Canale and Rudder with pay and would start an inquiry into the death of Reginald Talbert. The reporter also noted that the officers, especially Canale, could face criminal prosecution. In summary, the reporter observed that the death of Reginald Talbert had prompted considerable and rather immediate outcry in the project and that residents were organizing a demonstration in front of Metro police headquarters for Monday morning.

Continuing to drive north, Sally thought about the project killing and her own contact with the police earlier that morning. As a lawyer, Sally appreciated that police had considerable discretion. She also realized that it was impossible to provide a blueprint for every citizen-police interaction. However, she wondered about the Metro City case and was troubled when she recalled the report's description of deadly force.

"Why did the officer take such drastic actions," she asked out loud, "...couldn't he have done something short of that and why the repeated firings?" However trivial her own, earlier contact with the police, she wondered if things would have been different had she argued with the trooper or somehow resisted the ticket he really should have imposed. Should he have filed a report for the speed she was actually going? What made him write her up for a slower, and cheaper, speed? Would he have done the same thing if she had been speeding on a Saturday night? Although Sally's legal practice did not carry much criminal work or contact with criminal justice authorities, she thought about all of the day's police reports as she drove to her family and wondered what the average citizen thought about police discretion.

DISCUSSION QUESTIONS

1. Should the state trooper have filed a ticket for the full speed Cribari was driving? What do you think contributed to his decision to give Cribari a break?

2. What kind of enforcement does Cribari's contact with Trooper Wilson illustrate and how typical do you think the trooper's behavior was?

3. The shooting of Reginald Talbert obviously represents a far more serious exercise of police authority or discretion than Cribari's speeding. Considering this, how are the two situations similar? How are they different?
4. What might have prompted Canale to take such drastic action in the case of Reginald Talbert?
5. Do you think Canale's use of deadly force was justified? When should deadly force be used by police?
6. What do both of these incidents tell us about police discretion? Could such discretion be controlled? If so, how?

SUGGESTED READING
"MERCY, MERCY, LADY"

Atkins, Burton and Mark Pogrebin, Editors
   1982 *The Invisible Justice System: Discretion and the Law*. Cincinnati, Ohio: Anderson Publishing Company.

   One of a limited number of anthologies on discretion and its exercise in the Criminal Justice System. The editors offer chapters in five major sections: discretion in general; arrest; prosecution; courts and judges; and corrections, and include chapters by leading criminal justice scholars. Of particular interest are James Q. Wilson's article on police discretion and the editors' introduction on discretionary decision-making.

Davis, Kenneth Culp
   1971 *Discretionary Justice: A Preliminary Inquiry*. Urbana, Illinois: University of Illinois Press.

   A classic analysis of discretionary authority with particular emphasis on its exercise by police officers. Although the author's emphasis on administrative control and law may not meet with universal agreement, it stands as one of the first and still leading analyses of this element of justice.

Evans, Margaret, Editor
   1978 *Discretion and Control*. Beverly Hills, California: Sage Publications.

   An anthology on particular dimensions of the exercise of discretionary authority in criminal justice. Contributing authors focus on controlling the exercise of discretion through legislation and by the courts with additional attention to specific dimensions of correctional discretionary authority.

Goldstein, Joseph
   1960 "Police Discretion Not to Invoke the Criminal Process: Low-Visibility Decisions in the Administration of Justice." *Yale Law Journal* 69: 543-594.

   The classic analysis of police exercise of discretionary authority, this article directs the reader's attention to police decisions not to apply or enforce the criminal law. Goldstein puts considerable emphasis on the difference among alternate conceptions of law enforcement (total, full, actual).

Law and Contemporary Problems
   1984 Special Issue on Police Discretion. 47: 1-312. An entire journal issue devoted to police discretion.

Case Two

What Do We Do With 2,000 Streakers?

SATURDAY, SEPTEMBER 28

Chief Bill Burton was shaving on an unusually quiet Saturday morning when he was startled to hear the local deejay announce on the radio that a "streaking challenge" had been issued to all college students in University City. Burton stopped shaving and turned up the volume to make sure he heard it right. "OK, campers, this is your buddy, Uncle Luke, asking if you are going to let those 500 streakers in Columbia City set the standard for college boys and girls on the eastern seaboard? That's right, you heard me—are you going to take it? I mean, the Columbia kids actually bragged that nobody, nobody was going to put on a bigger streaking show. Are you men and women or Mickeys and Minnies?"

Burton paused after the deejay finished and observed to his wife that that was all he needed. "With five home football games still on the schedule, I don't need hundreds of naked students running all over campus." "Relax," Susan, Bob's wife, rejoined. "Our students won't take to the streets barebottom. I mean, they have more sense, don't they?"

SATURDAY, SEPTEMBER 28

The band in a local college hangout, O'Leary's, seemed to play at a thousand decibels, and hundreds of students milled about, drinking beer and, in some corners, dancing. During the break, the lead guitarist took the microphone and called out to the assembled students, "What are you going to do about Columbia City? Huh? Are you going to let those creeps lead the streaking game? I mean surely you can gather more than a measly 500 naked students, proud to bare their bottoms for University City!" By this time, the students had consumed a healthy amount of beer and picked up a chant, "We're number one! We're number one!" Thinking that winning had to be better defined, the band leader shouted, "Let's get thousands on the streets. Let's show them what University City is made of!"

Similar scenes erupted at several of the college bars all over town. Perhaps the absence of a home football game contributed to the contagion, as students responded to deejay and band leader suggestions that they take to the streets—naked of course.

SUNDAY SEPTEMBER 29

Late Sunday afternoon, a group of students gathered at a local fraternity to plan the streaking carnival. "First," observed one student, a junior, Michael Main, "we've got to get the word to all the houses: Saturday, October 5 is the day! We'll start on Pumpkin Avenue, run past the basketball arena, and then move on around the football stadium. We'll end up on Middle Avenue, at the big fraternity houses." Working at a speed that would impress their professors, the students xeroxed notices and sent pledges to deliver them to fraternity and sorority houses surrounding the campus. At the top, each notice proclaimed, "2,000 streakers! Let's get 2,000 streakers!"

By Sunday evening, Chief Bill Burton had received several telephone calls from his officers who had overheard the "streaking challenge" or picked up one of the notices about the October 5 schedule. Apparently, one zealous pledge took to posting them on telephone poles, street signs, and store windows! Campus officers helped to take the illegally posted signs down, but worried that they would be called on to deal with thousands of naked students. Therefore, the calls to Chief Burton.

Still later that evening, Chief Burton called his superior, campus public safety director, Ed Markowitz. "Ed, we may have a problem on our hands," Burton explained. "Have you heard these radio deejays challenge our students to streak by the thousands?" Ed replied that he had, but attributed it to typical deejay banter. "Surely, they aren't taking them seriously?" "Well," Burton went on, "notices setting Saturday, October 5 as 'Streaking Saturday' have been posted all over town. The fraternity and sorority houses seem to have taken the lead. My officers have pulled signs from telephone and street poles all around campus. They could pull this off. At least, we should be grateful that they didn't schedule it for football Saturday. But still, what are we going to do if 2,000 streakers take to the streets?"

MONDAY, SEPTEMBER 30

Early that morning Ed Markowitz and Bill Burton met to review the latest reports about "Streaking Saturday." By that time, the local newspapers were picking up on the story —with the two "dailies" giving the item front page attention. "Must be a slow news day," Ed observed, "for McConnell and Rupright (the editors of the local papers) to run this stuff on the first page." Additionally, virtually every deejay in a vicinity of 50 miles was periodically reminding his/her listeners that "Streaking Saturday" would soon be here. As one deejay put it, "Are you going to let it pass without you?"

By noon, the university president, Fred Ashmore, was on the phone to Markowitz. "Ed, I have already gotten four calls about this streaking business. Two parents want to know what I am going to do to stop it. One pastor complained about the degradation of student life and the general absence of morals, while the city police want to know how we intend to handle it. Chief Massey asked if we would need any of his officers." Ed chuckled to himself about Massey's offer as the university rarely asked the city police for backup on football Saturdays. Relying on campus officers from other schools, the university had quietly adopted a policy of keeping on friendly, but distant terms with the local city authorities—the balance between campus and city law enforcement was sometimes hard to maintain.

At a hastily called meeting, the president discussed the situation with his public safety director and chief of police. "I don't see how we can stop them," Ashmore observed. "Short of something akin to curfews and house arrest, we can't keep them off the streets." Markowitz and Burton both agreed, but emphasized that the situation was potentially explosive. "While it's different from football Saturday," Burton observed, "some of the same problems are there: large crowds that could easily get out of control, traffic headaches, angry citizens, and possible injuries to person and property. I just hope they streak in the early hours of the morning when alcohol consumption is likely to be low." "What if they start the night before," Markowitz thought out loud, "and simply party through the night?"

TUESDAY, OCTOBER 1

Chief Bill Burton assembled a small group of his staff to plan for security for the Saturday streaking extravaganza. Following Ed Markowitz's order to prepare "for a home football game," Burton gathered the heads of his major divisions to prepare for Saturday's streakers. Because the staff did not have a reliable estimate of the numbers of people streaking and watching, they elected to prepare for a large contingent. "Better safe than sorry," Chief Burton reasoned.

Burton reviewed the streaking route outlined in the flyers and the notices distributed all over campus and assigned particular officers and patrol cars for the start and finish of the parade. Particular points along the route were designated as "trouble spots" and officers were assigned to monitor them. Ambulances were put on call and a riot-equipped squad held in reserve in case things got out of hand. Calling off all vacations and leave time, Burton assigned every officer on his roster for Saturday duty. Although he worried about the overtime costs to the university, he thought he had no alternative. With large crowds a full force is needed. If not assembled, he reasoned, it could not be gathered at short notice—particularly if traffic were tied up and crowd control relaxed.

A major decision confronting Burton and his staff was the degree of law enforcement. As Burton observed to Markowitz, they could, theoretically, arrest any streaker for indecent exposure, but such an action not only was impossible but also highly inflammatory. Officers, Burton emphasized in his instructions, were only to make arrests for two things: obvious safety violation and violence to person or property.

With officer assignments set out, traffic control outlined, arrest instructions clarified, and emergency crews prepared in reserve, Burton held his breath and waited for Saturday. Although one student had taken to streaking at last year's commencement, no groups of students had run through the town barebottom, so Burton had no idea of what to expect.

SATURDAY, OCTOBER 5

The student organizers had set the streaking show for 11:00 a.m. About 8:00 a.m. the skies were clear and the weather forecast was promising, too promising, almost. The day's high was estimated at 68 degrees and the forecast called for sunny skies with virtually no wind. Although inclement weather would have created its own set of problems, clear skies were not exactly a blessing, at least in Chief Burton's mind. By 10:00 a.m., crowds of spectators had begun to gather at the key vantage points along the well-publicized route. These included the starting point on Pumpkin Avenue, the yard in front of the basketball arena, the bridge near the football stadium and student center, and the parking lots at the route's closure point. As Chief Burton looked over the crowds, he was amazed to see that a variety of townspeople were present. The crowd clearly was not drawn from the student ranks. Standing near the football stadium bridge was the president of the local chamber of commerce. Near the basketball arena were several local clergy, some with their families in tow. City council members, faculty, some prominent merchants, and even some "football fans" were gathering to watch the show. As Ed Markowitz observed to his officers, "You can't have a show without an audience." An audience was certainly gathering for the University City Streakers.

As the starting time of 11:00 a.m. moved closer, Burton reviewed his instructions with his field officers and reminded each that arrests were only necessary for obvious safety violations and violence to person and property. Although several citizens had called in to suggest massive arrests for public indecency, the department had no intention of such sweeps. Selective enforcement was also inadvisable because it would be hard to justify one arrest out of several hundreds. Such an action would also be likely to elicit an averse reaction from both the streakers and the crowd. "To be sure," Burton responded to one citizen, "the law does prohibit public indecency. But what can one police department do with 2,000 streakers?"

A campus patrol car moved ahead of the streakers as they gathered at the sorority and fraternity houses—moving slowly along the route that had been closed to traffic two hours earlier. Immediately behind the car was a female horseback rider with flowing black hair. Of course, the press dubbed her "Lady Godiva" and photos of her ride made excellent frontpage coverage in the next day's newspapers. Local editors, however, were cautious and allowed for closely cropped photos that focused only on the hair and head! Running after "Lady Godiva" were approximately 2,000 streakers. Primarily undergraduates, they moved along at a fairly good clip, although the balmy weather was not an incentive to haste. Perhaps a lingering sense of modesty prompted some to move hurriedly, but the majority ran at something less than a full jog. As the stream of students ran though the campus, the crowd sent up a huge cheer. For their part, the students seemed like young children at Christmas—elated with the attention they were receiving and somehow delighted at the novelty of a new toy.

Burton's officers watched cautiously, although many had difficulty suppressing grins at "Lady Godiva" and other participants. However, as the streakers wound their way through campus, several officers noticed a couple on a motorcycle. Obviously participating in the streaking show, the young man and woman rode at the end of the crowd, bringing up the rear, if you will. Enjoying some of the notoriety of "Lady Godiva," they waved to the crowd and drove carefully along the route—relishing the attention the crowd lavished. As the pair approached the end of the route, one of the officers noted that they were not wearing helmets—an obvious violation of a safety ordinance. At the end of the route, the pair was pulled over and issued citations. As it turned out, their tickets were the only ones issued that day.

EPILOGUE

Chief Burton relaxed Saturday evening—grateful that "Streaking Saturday" had come to a close with no serious injuries and no serious problems. Although he was not convinced that the resulting publicity would be favorable, he was relieved that they did not have to call on reserve riot personnel or ambulances. Furthermore, he was glad no one got hurt, intentionally or inadvertently. The ticket issued to the motorcycle pair could have been avoided, he supposed, but the couple did not seem disturbed and the crowd chuckled when the officer issued helmet violation tickets to a couple with no clothes.

The week after the "show," Ed Markowitz was still getting calls about the university's failure to enforce public decency laws and its general inability to prevent the entire spectacle. Talking to one agitated parent, Ed explained that there were several prominent citizens in the crowd. "Ministers, priests, rabbis, council members, lawyers, doctors, businessmen—they were all there. Some of them even had their families with them! If you don't have an audience, you don't have a show," he insisted and explained that when the campus police were faced with such public support for streaking, there was little the university could do to stop it. "We can't be parents, cops, and moral guardians all at the same time," he emphasized. "You have to realize that sometimes it is impossible to enforce the law; maybe even safer not to. With a situation like this, you have potentially explosive problems. We elected to handle them quietly and cautiously, in the hopes that nothing serious would erupt. Fortunately, it worked for us. Really, what would you do with 2,000 streakers?"

DISCUSSION QUESTIONS

1. What atypical problem did the Campus Police Department have to deal with? What similar atypical problems do police departments occasionally face?
2. How is this law enforcement situation unusual? What demands does the situation make on the police agency, the officers, the community?
3. Should the police have let the students run through town naked? Could the police have stopped the streaking?
4. Should we limit police responsibility to exclude such atypical situations as campus streaking? Should police responsibility be expanded?
5. What other groups or sectors of society have a responsibility for situations like the campus streaking? To what extent are the police limited when those groups do or do not exercise restraint?

SUGGESTED READING
"WHAT DO WE DO WITH 2,000 STREAKERS?"

Goldstein, Herman
    1977 *Policing a Free Society*. Cambridge, Massachusetts: Ballinger Publishing Company.
    An analysis of the fundamental issues confronting police in American society. Particular emphasis is placed on issues related to public service and to the integrated nature of policing and its problems.

Muir, William Ker, Jr.
    1977 *Police: Streetcorner Politicians*. Chicago, Illinois: University of Chicago Press.
    A classic analysis of policing and the exercise of authority. Muir provides a rich theoretical and philosophical background for his analysis of discretionary authority and grounds his study in extensive interviews with a small number of police officers.

Radelet, Louis A. and Hoyt Coe Reed
    1980 *The Police and the Community*. Encino, California: Glencoe Publishing Company.
    The third edition of a classic textbook on police community relations. The authors consider the police function in the community from psychological, sociological, and programmatic perspectives, and review a variety of issues related to the role of police in contemporary society.

Wilson, James Q.
    1968 *Varieties of Police Behavior: The Management of Law and Order in Eight Communities*. Cambridge, Massachusetts: Harvard University Press.
    Wilson's often-quoted analysis of three competing styles of law enforcement, this treatment of order maintenance, service, and enforcement strategies serves as a benchmark in the study of alternate approaches to policing.

Wilson, James Q. and George L. Kelling
    1988 "Broken Windows: The Police and Neighborhood Safety." In George F. Cole, Ed., *Criminal Justice: Law and Politics*. Pacific Grove, California: Brooks/Cole: 103-116.
    Reprinted from a 1982 issue of *Atlantic Monthly*, this article offers a reexamination of the role of police in contemporary society. The authors argue that police strategy should focus on order maintenance and accountability to the larger community.

Case Three

But It Was an Accident

TUESDAY, JANUARY 19: 2:OO A.M.

The winter chill had set in this southeastern college town, rather typical for January nights. Although the temperature had not dropped below freezing, it was cold, and a rather blustery wind made it seem colder. Officer Jackson Russom, Jack to family and friends, was patrolling the offices and buildings adjacent to the center of the city. Checking for signs of prowlers and burglars, Russom drove slowly around the parking lots surrounding the buildings and offices. As he approached the buildings occupied by a local fan and stove company, he thought he saw something near one of the buildings. Since the driveway moved around the building at a decreasing slope, he drove slowly to make sure that he didn't scare anyone off and to check against the possibility of foul play. As he drove through the parking lot, Russom was startled when he felt his car hit something. Instinctively, he stopped and put the car in reverse. At that moment, Russom realized with a fright that the object felt and sounded like a body. Quickly stopping the car and moving out, he saw a young man on the ground, obviously injured! Russom called immediately for an ambulance and a police backup. Within minutes, the ambulance attendants arrived and carefully examined the young man, who looked about twenty-five. Bearded and clothed in dark jacket and pants, he was unconscious. The ambulance attendants worried about serious injury.

After the ambulance had taken the as yet unidentified young man to the hospital, the police backup helped Russom file a report. Explaining that he was checking for a possible burglary, Russom emphasized that he did not see anyone standing in the road. More emphatically he insisted that he could not have spotted someone and then proceeded to drive over the person! Rather, Russom recounted he was making a routine patrol around the fan and stove company when he felt that he had driven over something. Driving back, he felt the same thing and then realized to his horror that the object could be a person.

TUESDAY, JANUARY 19: 8:00 A.M.

Local hospital personnel spent a frantic early morning with the unidentified young man whom Officer Russom had run over. Unconscious when he was brought to the hospital, he had regained consciousness and murmured incoherently that he had been taking a nap. Hospital personnel examined the damage to the spinal cord and estimated permanent paralysis. They waited, however, for additional expert consultation. Disturbed, they also noted that the injured man had a substantially high alcohol content, well over the .10 legal minimum. To complicate matters, they found no identification and consequently had no one to call. Local newspapers, however, ran the story on the morning edition's front page and soon the hospital and police department were flooded with calls from worried people who feared the injured could be a son or brother. More conclusive identification came later in the afternoon when a prominent local politician stopped by the hospital to see if her brother had been brought in. Calling his apartment, she became worried when she received no answer, especially since they were supposed to meet for breakfast the morning of the 19th.

Susan Shivy was a city councilwoman with over three terms in that position. As a partner in a local printing company, she had been active in local politics for some time, first as a member of the League of Women Voters and then as a Democratic party stalwart. Shivy still managed her printing company, but devoted considerable energy to her position on the city council. A zealous advocate of historical preservation and spokesperson for the more liberal wing of the council, she gained particular attention when she opposed a recent bill to limit the hours alcohol could be served in bars and restaurants in the city.

Shivy checked the hospital and identified her brother, Vic, as the man who had been severely injured in the early hours of the morning. Disturbed, she immediately called the police department to learn the identity of the officer and to see what kind of report he had filed.

Hospital personnel told her that Vic's prospects were not good. In fact, the specialist emphasized that he thought permanent paralysis was the best they could hope for. Shivy was disconsolate, her brother was her only sibling. Their parents had died in a plane crash several years earlier, and she assumed the parental role. As a consequence, she was constantly looking out for Vic. In fact, Susan was the one who pushed him to graduate school when he seemed uncertain about joining her in the printing business. Although he was not enthusiastic about his graduate work in psychology, he liked the graduate student lifestyle. Requiring little to live on, he rented a small, cramped apartment in the center of the city and routinely visited friends and lounged in local bars during the week. The evening of January 18, Vic had visited one such friend. Their evening continued long past the basketball game they were watching on TV as Vic started home around 1:30 a.m. As Vic's friend would later tell a court, they had consumed a large amount of beer. Steve, Vic's friend, wasn't too concerned about this because Vic had walked over to his place and would, no doubt, return home the same way. How could he get hurt on his feet, Steve reasoned.

WEDNESDAY, JANUARY 20: 9:30 A.M.

Police Chief Chandler called Jackson Russom into his office. Although Russom was still assigned to the "graveyard shift," Chandler insisted he stop by his office that morning to talk with him about the accident. Chandler was visibly upset. The local newspapers gave the story considerable attention, but the reporter neglected to emphasize several details that Chandler thought were essential to the department's case. First, there was no mention of Shivy's dark clothing. More importantly there was no description of his intoxication. A reader taking the newspaper story at face value would assume that Shivy was simply taking a shortcut to his city apartment when a patrol officer drove too quickly around a deserted building, mowed him down, and then proceeded to make matters worse by putting the car in reverse and repeating the action. Chandler asked Russom to review the details in his report one more time, and then proceeded to tell him that the department would take care of this. Russom, Chandler emphasized, was to go nowhere near Shivy or his sister. At least not for now.

Leaving the chief's office, Russom did not think he could go back home and sleep. To be sure, he was tired and exhausted—physically and emotionally. The sound of his car moving over Shivy's body haunted him and he wondered if he would ever have any peace. Reading the newspaper accounts, even some family and friends observed that they didn't think he could have done such a thing.

Russom decided that he needed to see Shivy and to apologize for the injury. He also wanted to tell him that it was an accident—he simply didn't see him and was certain he was laying on the parking lot. At the hospital, Susan Shivy was standing near her brother's hospital room door. She barely managed to spit out the words, "So you're the murderer." "But he isn't dead," Russom emphasized. "He may as well be," Susan rejoined. Russom asked if he could see Vic, but Susan refused and observed with an obvious curtness that he could see him in court.

JANUARY 29

Lawyers for Vic Shivy filed papers in Superior Court and the case of Shivy v. Russom was on! In the civil litigation, the plaintiff asked for compensatory damages of $2.1 million and a punitive award of $1.5 million. Russom was startled when the Chief told him about the lawsuit. "They are really going to sue me! But it was an accident!" The Chief was equally bothered and told Russom that he and the city attorney were thinking about an out of court settlement. "We could settle for a lot less than half a million and avoid the whole trial," Chandler stressed. Russom couldn't believe his ears—settle. "But why? I didn't do anything wrong. It was an accident. The guy was dead-drunk and had to be lying in the parking lot. Do you really think I was looking for sprawling drunks patrolling the fan and stove place that night?"

Leaving the chief's office, Russom called on an old friend, attorney John Blasingame. Blasingame wasn't the flamboyant type. Although very successful in criminal and civil litigation, he won juries with his soft-spoken, gentle manner and his tenacity. When his secretary told him that Russom was in his office but had no appointment, Blasingame called him in and observed that the past week must have been trying. Russom nodded and proceeded to tell Blasingame about the chief's preference for an out of court settlement. "They don't seem willing to try," Russom observed. "Do I have any alternative? I mean Shivy's named me *and* the police department in the suit." Blasingame told Russom to calm down and suggested they adjourn to a quiet restaurant where he could review the nature of the litigation Russom was likely to face.

Over lunch, Blasingame explained that police conduct has increasingly become the subject of tort litigation. Explaining that torts were personal injuries like false arrest, invasion of privacy, and defamation, Blasingame reviewed the actions typically covered by state and federal law. "Since Shivy is pursuing litigation in state court [The Superior Court is the state's major, trial court for both criminal and civil actions.], he is obviously going to sue for negligent conduct." "Under the common law," Blasingame continued, "state tort actions are either intentional or negligent. Intentional torts include those situations where the police engage in voluntary acts that he/she knows are likely to produce certain physical consequences. Negligence, on the other hand, stems more from carelessness where the officer is not certain about the outcome of his/her actions, but realizes that there is a foreseeable risk." "You," Blasingame emphasized, "are probably being sued for negligence. I suspect that Shivy's attorney will argue that you should have been careful and, even if you could not have seen the victim, you should not have driven over the body/object in reverse." "What isn't so clear to me," Blasingame reasoned, "is why the suit includes your department. Usually, you have to establish that the department (meaning your boss) negligently employed you, didn't train you properly, or didn't provide adequate supervision. It seems to me that your situation doesn't fit here."

Russom thought for a while and observed that he had a history of driving accidents prior to his employment as a police officer. "Do you suppose that will be raised to justify the extension of the suit to the department? And who helps me? Should I hire my own attorney, or work with the city attorney? Who will defend the department? What a mess!" In response, Blasingame told Russom to take it easy. He would check the suit and defend him if need be. Russom should, though, check with his chief to see if they were still intent on settling out of court.

FEBRUARY 3

Chief Chandler was talking with the city attorney about the Russom case. "I think we should settle," the attorney advised. "The publicity with a case like this is going to be terrible, the cost of litigation substantial, and I don't think we can win. I mean, the guy will come into the courtroom in a wheelchair. You know what the jury's going to do. We don't stand a chance. Do you think you can convince Russom to go along with this. He seemed pretty adamant that it was an accident and that he didn't do anything wrong." Chief Chandler hesitated. "I'm not sure," he said. "I'll have to talk with him."

Later that afternoon, Chandler did talk to Russom. He explained that the city wanted to settle out of court and emphasized that he thought they would lose if they went to trial. Shivy's just looking for a few bucks anyway and the city would rather cut its losses now than risk a huge damage award later. Chandler had some foundation for his concern about high damages. Although police in small departments are infrequently subject to civil litigation, such suits have increased and some jury decisions have exceeded one million dollars. Russom emphasized that he was not going to settle. If the city wanted to, fine, but he would pursue the case and pay for his own attorney if need be. "It simply was not my fault," Russom insisted. "Shivy was dead drunk and sprawled in the middle of a parking lot at 2:00 in the morning. Give me a break."

SEPTEMBER 1

Several months passed before the case of Shivy v. Russom *and* the police department came up for trial. In the interim, both sides prepared diligently. Shivy's attorney played on the negligence dimension and hoped that Russom's history of driving accidents would help the jury conclude that he was negligent in driving and the Police Department in hiring. If they did hire him, they shouldn't have put him behind the wheel of a patrol car. On the other side, Russom's attorney (his friend Blasingame) worked with the city attorney for the plaintiff's case. Chandler had acquiesced to litigation when he realized that Russom was not going to settle. "We may as well hope for the best," he reasoned. Russom and his boss were arguing that the responsibility for the tragedy—and they acknowledged that it was a tragedy—was Shivy's. Had he been sober and upright, Russom would have seen him and been able to stop. Russom drove very slowly when patrolling the businesses and office districts near downtown. Obviously you could not take those parking lots at high speed.

The trial started with the selection of the jury. Both sides moved in quick but predictable ways. The plaintiffs struck those with relatives and friends in policing and those who admitted to driving accidents. The defense tried to stay away from elderly women, college students (undergraduate and graduate) and those with family and friends who had been injured in car accidents. As the day's proceedings came to a close, Officer Russom approached Shivy and asked if he could speak to him. Confined to a wheelchair, Shivy appeared bitter and somewhat perplexed. Nonetheless, he did agree to speak with Russom, much against the advice of all attorneys. "I'm really sorry," Russom said, "really sorry. I simply didn't see you. It was an accident."

SEPTEMBER 8

The trial went on for five days. Witnesses were brought in who testified to Shivy's injury and who emphasized the permanence of the paralysis. Supplementing this was the testimony of physical therapists who described in great detail the difficulty Vic would have in simply taking care of routine day-to-day functions. Additionally, the plaintiffs introduced Russom's driving record, claiming that the department should not have hired him or put him in a patrol car.

Russom's attorneys countered most points and emphasized that Shivy was well over the legal limit for intoxication. Arguing that he was lying down on the parking lot, they emphasized that no reasonable person could be expected to look for drunks on the ground of a parking lot at 2:00 a.m. when patrolling for burglaries. On this point of Shivy's location, the two sides were in conflict. Shivy testified that he was crouching not laying, while Russom countered that even that would have been difficult to see.

Eventually, the case went to the jury. Deliberating for five hours, they concluded that Russom had not been negligent and rendered a verdict in the defendant's favor. Russom was relieved though still visibly drawn over the ordeal. As he approached Shivy, his attorney heard him whisper, "I live with this every day. I live with this every day and wish it hadn't happened. Please understand that."

DISCUSSION QUESTIONS

1. Was Officer Russom at fault in the injury that Vic Shivy suffered?
2. Should Officer Russom be held criminally responsible for the injury?
3. What are the merits in Shivy's civil suit?
4. Do you agree with the jury's verdict? If so, why? If not, what would you have done?
5. Did Russom's supervisors act in a responsible fashion? Should they have supported Russom in his efforts to take the civil suit to trial?
6. What contributes to such civil suits and what impact do you think they have on society as a whole, police departments, and individual citizens?
7. What recourse do citizens have outside of civil suits when they think they have been unfairly treated or seriously injured by police actions?

SUGGESTED READING
"BUT IT WAS AN ACCIDENT"

Barrineau, H. E., III

1987   *Civil Liability in Criminal Justice*. Cincinnati, Ohio: Anderson Publishing Company.

A summary analysis of civil liability in general, its application to criminal justice processes, Section 1983, and current trends. Since the greatest number of lawsuits filed against criminal justice practitioners is raised in federal courts, the extended discussion of Section 1983 is especially useful.

Call, Jack and Donald Slesnick

1983   "Legal Aspects of Police Administration." In Charles R. Swanson and Leonard Territo, *Police Administration: Structures, Processes, and Behavior*. New York: Macmillan Publishing Company: 295-334.

An extensively referenced chapter on the legal dimensions of police administration and management. Call and Slesnick offer a useful analysis of liability for police conduct, administrative discipline, the constitutional rights of police, and related issues of discipline and employment.

Hardy, Paul T. and J. Devereux Weeks

    1985   *Personal Liability of Public Officials Under Federal Law*. Athens, Georgia: University of Georgia Institute of Government.

    A concise description and analysis of potential liability under Section 1983 and a review of major court decisions. Selected topics include qualified immunity, liability for negligence, and liability for subordinates' actions.

Schmidt, Wayne

    1974   *Survey of Police Misconduct Litigation: 1967-1971*. Evanston, Illinois: Americans for Effective Law Enforcement.

    Report of a survey of all law enforcement agencies in the United States with ten or more sworn officers. Approximately half of the departments surveyed responded, yielding a fairly comprehensive picture of the status of related litigation.

Roth, R. P.

    1988   "The Present State of Governmental Immunity." *Michigan Bar Journal* 67: 30.

    A summary of current law regarding immunity of governmental authorities.

Case Four

Hard Time Finding Charlie

PART ONE

Riverton was one of the state's oldest cities. Built on the banks of the Orogamee River, it had been a military outpost and trading center in its early days and was now a center of commerce for a large two-state area. In the center of the downtown commercial district was Veterans' Square, a large "green space" around which some of the city's oldest and most established businesses were located. This was the sector of the city that was patrolled by Sgt. Steve Boyle and his six-member squad.

Charlie Maxwell, a member of Boyle's squad, had recorded several months of much improved patrol activity. Recently, however, Sgt. Boyle had begun to perceive that Charlie's old habits were catching up with him. A year earlier, Sgt. Boyle warned Maxwell to take steps to improve his appearance, his health, and especially his professionalism. Boyle had hoped that a general revitalization of the officer might effectively eliminate several specific problems that made the patrolman's job performance marginal at best. Now, however, Boyle was beginning to see evidence of backsliding. The firm conviction that Charlie was drinking on duty again was particularly troublesome. Sgt. Boyle decided a confrontation was in order when he noted Maxwell's wrinkled and soiled uniform at the close of a morning roll call.

"Charlie, let me tell you something. There isn't going to be a next time if I catch you drinking while you're on duty. You look bad, you smell even worse, and your work just isn't up to par. You need to do something about this situation, and you need to do it right away."

"Ah, Sarge, give me a break," Maxwell replied. "I just overslept a little this morning and didn't have time to get all dolled up. My 'drinking problem' is all in your head. Have you ever seen me drinking on the job?" "No, not yet," retorted Boyle. "But I'm sure I will. In fact, I'm positive that sooner or later I'm going to catch you in the act when you and I least expect it. I'm not pulling any 'chicken' number on you either.

23

I have no intention of sneaking around checking up on you. You're going to flaunt it because I don't think you can help yourself. One of these days I'm going to be there to see it. So watch out!"

Sgt. Boyle was a member of the "new breed" of professional police officers that the Riverton Police Department had recruited in recent years. College-educated, Boyle had risen in the ranks faster than virtually any of the older officers in the department. Passionately dedicated to police professionalism, Boyle was powerfully resented by many of the "old hands." The more senior members of the department, especially those in the uniformed division, resented the erosion of a style of policing that had characterized the police department for many years. This older style was being replaced by a professional model of law enforcement being carried out by a younger, better educated, and highly motivated group of officers. During Boyle's rookie year, Charlie Maxwell had taken great pride in pointing out to him that his initials, "S.B.," stood for "School Boy." Now, four years later, the 25-year-old patrol sergeant was Maxwell's immediate supervisor.

The style of police work that was most congenial to Charlie Maxwell rested on a unique set of assumptions. Maxwell had been with the Riverton Police Department for 21 years and had never risen above the rank of patrolman. He had exerted most of his effort toward creating a nest for himself in Riverton's central business district. Maxwell subscribed to a normative system that placed a very high value on a "personalistic" style of enforcement. He had always treated the downtown area as turf. Behavior that he sought to sanction was sanctioned; behavior that he chose to ignore was ignored. The special "favors" that were extended to Charlie by downtown businessmen were repaid through enhanced surveillance of particular businesses and a general laxity in the enforcement of ordinances (e.g., various parking restrictions) that were disadvantageous to particular interests. By the time of Sgt. Boyle's assignment to the central business district, Maxwell was so involved in petty graft and corruption that he had secured the keys to between 25 and 30 businesses where he was free to enter and help himself to the "goodies" that shopkeepers made available to him.

Maxwell was not accustomed to providing supervisory personnel with information on his travels during his beat. This, of course, enhanced his ability to "graze" on the sundry rewards that the downtown area had to offer. On one occasion, Boyle had such difficulty finding Maxwell that he literally had to go door-to-door in an effort to determine the patrolman's whereabouts. He finally located Maxwell at one of Riverton's most elegant hotels. Boyle found him in the restaurant kitchen standing by a stove with a 16 oz. T-bone steak on the griddle and a basket of french fries broiling in a deep fat fryer. Charlie was even wearing a chef's apron over his uniform. When Boyle questioned what he was doing, Maxwell asserted glibly, "I'm cooking my supper, Sarge. What do think I'm doing?"

Subsequent to this encounter, Sgt. Boyle became aware of Charlie's key collection and ordered him to return all the keys he had in his possession to their owners with the strict injunction that he discontinue the practice of accepting gratuities from local businessmen. Although Maxwell protested vehemently, he had little choice but to return most of the keys. A key to the front entrance of the Avondale Finance and Loan Company was one of a select few that were not returned.

On Sunday afternoon, Sgt. Boyle was returning to police headquarters to drop off a folder of reports destined for the department's administrative services division. What began as a routine trip to the station changed, however, as the prophecy Sgt. Boyle had foretold earlier came to pass unexpectedly.

As Boyle headed north on Central Avenue, he glanced diagonally across the open expanses of Veterans' Square. Since Sunday afternoon traffic in the downtown area was sparse as usual, he had little difficulty seeing patrolman Charlie Maxwell's traffic scooter parked on Second Street in front of the Avondale Finance and Loan Company. Sgt. Boyle could tell that Charlie was not on the scooter, but why had Maxwell not radioed that he was out of service? Where was he? Boyle decided to drive around the block to see if he could locate the officer.

At the corner of Second and Central, Sgt. Boyle turned east and drove slowly along the side of the street where Charlie had parked the scooter. When he pulled in front of Avondale Finance, Boyle caught sight of Maxwell standing near the center of a large picture window inside the building. Boyle could not believe what he saw. With his head thrown back and his elbow pointed toward the ceiling, Maxwell was polishing off the last of a can of beer quite oblivious to the world around him. Boyle stopped long enough for Maxwell to catch a glimpse of the patrol car. Maxwell's eyes bulged, the beer can frozen to his lips, as he too realized that Sgt. Boyle's prophecy had just now come true. Boyle returned a scowl and then proceeded around Veterans' Square to decide what he should do next.

PART TWO

Upon leaving his patrol car, Boyle found that the entrance to Avondale Finance was unlocked, although all downtown businesses were supposed to be closed on Sundays. Officer Maxwell was seated behind a desk several feet from the front door of the building.

"Hi, Sarge," Maxwell cheerily exclaimed. "How ya doin'?"

Boyle did not respond as he passed Maxwell on his way to a storeroom at the rear of the business. There, Boyle found a refrigerator; he was not terribly surprised to find the appliance filled with cold beer. As Boyle returned to the desk where the patrolman was seated he noticed three or four empty beer cans in the wastepaper basket beside the desk. The can on top was still wet from the beads of condensation that had formed on its exterior.

"Been doing a little paperwork, Charlie?" Boyle inquired. Maxwell replied, "Right, Sarge. Just trying to get caught up."

"Does the paperwork go a little better with a few beers under your belt?" asked Boyle in a captious and unsympathetic tone.

"Sarge, I don't know what you're talking about," Maxwell responded innocently.

"Don't play games with me, Charlie. Neither one of us is that big a fool," said Boyle. "I told you this day would come. Now it's arrived and we need to decide where we go from here."

Steve Boyle spun about and headed for the front door of the finance company. As he reached the door he turned to Patrolman Maxwell, "I want to see you back at the station immediately."

Sgt. Boyle radioed Lt. Carlson, shift commander of the patrol squads, and asked Carlson to meet him in the parking lot at headquarters. Outside the station, Boyle was explaining the situation to Lt. Carlson when Maxwell arrived on the traffic scooter.

"What kind of bull are you spreadin' about me now?" Maxwell belligerently inquired.

Carlson intervened before Boyle could respond. "What's this I hear about you drinking on duty?"

"That's a downright lie. He's been laying for me ever since I transferred to the downtown squad," retorted Maxwell.

"If that's the case," Boyle responded, "you won't mind stepping inside for a blood alcohol test."

Reaching for his service revolver, Maxwell exclaimed, "I'll blow your damn head off!"

Boyle responded, almost instinctively, by reaching for his weapon. Carlson moved quickly to head off further trouble by stepping between the two officers while at the same time grabbing Maxwell by the wrist. "Hold it!" he shouted. "Hold it right there."

Patrolman Maxwell was disarmed and escorted into the station by Lt. Carlson. In Carlson's office, Maxwell was ordered to take a breathalyzer test to detect if he had been drinking. He refused to cooperate at first, but then was given a choice of "voluntarily" taking the test or being summarily dismissed for refusing to obey a direct order from a superior officer. The results of the test showed him to have a blood alcohol content of .09 percent, $\frac{1}{100}$ of a percent below legal intoxication. Maxwell was sent home with a suspension pending formal proceedings in his case.

Departmental administrators found themselves facing the first serious disciplinary challenge to "professionalism" as it was now defined within the department. They had before them a clear-cut example of the very type of conduct that they sought to root out in the interest of professional law enforcement and it presented an obvious threat to the integrity of the departmental chain of command. The actions that Sgt. Boyle had taken were completely appropriate and unquestionably in the best interest of public safety. Yet, the offending party was nearly old enough to be his immediate supervisor's father. Further, the administrators realized that to dismiss Maxwell would be to deny a 21-year veteran of the department his right to retirement benefits; the mere filing of formal charges against Maxwell had already had a debilitating effect on the morale of the older officers. Reaching a decision in this case would not be easy.

DISCUSSION QUESTIONS

1. Early in the case Sgt. Boyle confronts Charlie Maxwell with his suspicion that the officer is engaging in "old habits" of misconduct. Do you feel that Boyle's decision to confront Maxwell directly is an appropriate one? Is there an alternative approach that might be more effective?

2. In some respects, the relationship between Boyle and Maxwell is indicative of strained relations between younger and older officers generally. What are the cultural, structural, and interpersonal sources of tension between these two groups? If you were an administrator in the Riverton Police Department what steps might you take to reduce tension within the patrol ranks?

3. What is your assessment of the special "favors" that local business people extended to officers such as Charlie Maxwell? Do you feel that these favors were freely extended or were there strings attached? Where does one draw the line between tokens of appreciation on the one hand, and evidence of graft and corruption on the other?

4. The evidence presented in this case clearly indicates that Officer Maxwell is guilty of drinking while on duty. How should the departmental administrators handle this situation? Do you see this case presenting a legitimate dilemma between police professionalism and the need to protect the dignity and self-respect of older officers? What would be the implications of firing Officer Maxwell compared to other alternatives?

5. In general, is it more appropriate to think of Charlie Maxwell's problems as personal deficiencies or as outcomes of the type of police culture in which he has served for 21 years?

SUGGESTED READING
"HARD TIME FINDING CHARLIE"

City of New York, Commission to Investigate Allegations of Police Corruption and the City's Anti-Corruption Procedures

1973 *The Knapp Commission Report on Police Corruption. New York: Braziller.*

In the early 1970s the Knapp Commission made a major contribution to the study of corruption in urban law enforcement. The Commission noted that the major form of corrupt practices was of the "grass-eating" variety; minor patterns of deviance similar to the many gratuities that were extended to Charlie Maxwell. In addition to the documentation of wide-spread corruption, the Commission offered numerous recommendations designed to reduce corrupt activity.

Robinette, Hillary

1987 *Burnout in Blue: Managing the Police Marginal Performer.* New York: Praeger.

A major source of problem behavior on the part of police officers is burnout. This study generates a sophisticated model for identifying a variety of problem behaviors related to burnout, and outlines a number of strategies that police administrators can use to minimize levels of marginal performance within law enforcement.

Smith, Alexander, Bernard Locke and Abe Fenster

1970 "Authoritarianism in Policemen Who are College Graduates and Non-College Police." *Journal of Criminal Law, Criminology, and Police Science.* 61: 313-315.

Do police officers who have college degrees tend to be more authoritarian than their non-college peers? In this study of the effects of college education on police, Smith et al. conclude that police officers with baccalaureate degrees tend to be less authoritarian than officers without degrees. Also of interest, however, older officers in both educational categories had lower authoritarianism levels than younger officers.

Stoddard, Ellwyn R.

1968   "Informal 'Code' of Police Deviance: A Group Approach to Blue-Coat Crime." *Journal of Criminal, Criminology, and Police Science.* 59: 201-213.

This study contrasts the explanation of police deviancy as a problem of individual corruption with the notion that corruption is also a product of group interaction. Particularly significant is the identification and documentation of a group "code" within police ranks that provides a cover for unlawful behavior.

Van Maanen, John

1983.   "The Boss: First-line Supervision in an American Police Agency." p. 275-317 in M. Punch (ed.) *Control in the Police Organizations.* Cambridge, MA: MIT Press.

This article is about the organizational role of police sergeants. Van Maanen points out that sergeants are the "personification" of internal control within police departments. The study describes how this role is performed including a discussion of the interaction between sergeants and the officers under their supervision.

Violanti, John M., James R. Marshall and Barbara Howe

1985   "Stress, Coping, and Alcohol Use: The Police Connection." *Journal of Police Science and Administration.* 13: 106-110.

This article identifies factors that influence alcohol use by police officers. The authors find that job stress to a greater extent than emotional dissonance and cynicism has the major impact on alcohol consumption. The authors discuss the social acceptability of alcohol use among police officers as a convenient method of coping with the vexations of police work.

Case Five

We've Got a Serious Problem Here

As state trooper Tom Green left the Deerfield County courthouse, he knew how the camel who had carried the "last straw" must have felt. Why was Hurdlow Tipps so terribly concerned about state air surveillance in the western part of the county? It was true that the state police used aircraft to spot speeders on state highways and it was also true they were now being used on a limited basis in Deerfield County. But Route 21 through the western part of the county wound through the foothills of the mountains where it was almost impossible to get above 35 m.p.h. in a car and would be extremely hazardous to patrol from the air. This part of the county had never been patrolled in this fashion. Mr. Tipps knew this; something else must be on his mind.

Green suspected that Tipps and Sheriff Cooper were involved in criminality that went beyond the petty stuff he had already been exposed to during the first six months he had been assigned to patrol in Deerfield. He already knew that the sheriff tolerated small-time bootlegging in the county and often used intimidation to remain the undisputed power in the county. He also was aware that Cooper was a "business" associate of Hurdlow Tipps. Today's meeting with Tipps and Cooper was not unlike the numerous other calls Green had received in recent weeks. Several times he had been summoned to the sheriff's office like an errant child to have a "chat," wherein the sheriff would alternately use solicitation and intimidation as a means of trying to get Green acclimated to the "Cooper Method" of law enforcement. Trooper Green decided it was time to visit Whit Jackson and see if he had any ideas about what was going on between Tipps and Cooper.

Agent Whit Jackson of the State Criminal Investigation Bureau (CIB) held a very different opinion of Sheriff Cooper than some of the citizens of Deerfield County. He had suspected for a long time that Cooper was a corrupt sheriff, but lacked sufficient hard evidence against him that could be used to seek a warrant for his arrest. Nevertheless he had directly experienced Cooper's arrogance and abusive treatment of officers from other agencies. Many times he had been berated by the sheriff in front of local citizens. It was also the sheriff's habit to call Jackson when he had gotten word that a CIB agent passed through, or had been in the county. "I understand that ya'll came through Tuesday afternoon 'bout 2:15 p.m.," he would say. "Ya'll oughta stop by when you're in Deerfield. You state boys need to learn some manners," he would exclaim. Cooper also never let Jackson forget that he was an "outsider" to Deerfield County even though he grew up in DeSoto Wells which was less than 60 miles from Deerfield.

As Green and Jackson talked, the latter indicated that the closest he had come to getting something concrete on Cooper involved an incident in which a woman from Deerfield County had called to report her suspicion that the Sheriff was running a protection racket in which he took kickbacks from drug dealers in order to make Deerfield County "safe" for drug trafficking. Jackson recalled that when he interviewed the woman at her home, a good twelve miles out in the county, she was so fearful of Cooper that she whispered throughout the entire interview. After the initial interview, the woman refused to provide any further cooperation. Without collaborating evidence, Jackson lacked probable cause to move on either the sheriff or the alleged drug dealers. In retrospect, it struck Jackson as odd that the sheriff had armed his deputies to the teeth in order to "take down" the ne'er-do-wells who were supposedly poisoning Deerfield County youth. Although he cussed Jackson up and down when he was told there was no basis to pursue the investigation, the sheriff looked surprisingly relieved as Jackson prepared to leave the county.

Jackson and Green agreed that they should immediately seek state authorization to open an investigation of Cooper and Tipps and do the very thing Hurdlow Tipps had warned Green not to do. The authorization was received and the air surveillance of Hurdlow Tipps's farm yielded very interesting results. About five hundred yards from a logging road nestled between a rocky escarpment and several hundred acres of woods, state agents discovered one and a half acres of highly cultivated marijuana growing on Tipps's farm. This permitted state agents to begin concentrated surveillance of the crop in order to link the marijuana to its actual owners. Realizing that Sheriff Cooper probably would not enter the field himself, Tom Green agreed to be "wired" with a hidden tape recorder and to indicate to Cooper a willingness to learn the "Cooper Method" of law enforcement.

The field surveillance took over a year to complete. During the first summer of surveillance CIB agents staked out the marijuana field from 9:00 p.m. until 6:00 a.m. Unfortunately, the entire field was harvested not long after surveillance had begun and the agents were not able to gather sufficient evidence for an indictment. During their second season on the site, agents literally camped out 24 hours a day and, in time, were able to take pictures of several hired hands working the crop. The big catch was a number of pictures of none other than Hurdlow Tipps fertilizing and cultivating his marijuana plants.

The major evidence against Earl Cooper was obtained through the use of the listening device carried by Trooper Green. Green had no difficulty securing the sheriff's confidence; the sheriff couldn't imagine that anyone wouldn't want a part of his action.

In the tapes of conversations between Cooper, Green, and others, Cooper spoke openly and frequently of his intention to cash in on the marijuana crop. He once confided to Green that "A man has gotta make it while he can. I intend to retire in another year or so and I aim to have a nice little nest egg. If I can't buy me a little grass shack in Hi-why-a [Hawaii], then I'll jest have to get me a condo! Two things, boy: don't you ever let the people see you living better than they do, and you always pay your taxes on everything you earn. The Feds ain't interested in how you earn your money, they jest want their cut of the action."

Evidence gathering against Cooper and Tipps reached a climax when CIB agents harvested the marijuana. On an August evening while Cooper and Tipps were hosting a cookout for a local political candidate, state agents filled three dump trucks with over 1,000 pounds of freshly cut marijuana. The crop had a street value of approximately $400,000. It was no wonder, therefore, that Hurdlow Tipps's jaw dropped to the ground the next morning when he paid a visit to an empty field. He sped back to the courthouse to call an emergency meeting of all the players involved in the conspiracy. Trooper Green and his tape recorder were also invited to witness Sheriff Earl Cooper lose his cool disposition.

EPILOGUE

There was considerable jocularity in evidence as Earl Cooper, Hurdlow Tipps, and three other defendants in the Deerfield County drug case gathered in the office of Snyder Weems, Cooper's attorney. Having already previewed the cassette tapes that had been released on discovery from the district attorney's office, Weems found little justification for lightheartedness.

As Weems started the tape recorder he exclaimed, "You asked for it, boys, and now you've got it." The tape began with a conversation between Cooper, Tipps, two sheriff's deputies, and Trooper Green that occurred the same morning that Tipps had discovered his denuded marijuana field. The relevant portion of the tape was a raging diatribe by Earl Cooper.

"We've got a serious problem here! I mean to tell ya' . . . we've got a *serious* problem here! That's my dope and I plan to get it back. It's that low-life Clements, or it's Puss Tolley—he's always been three inches lower than a snake's belly—no, maybe it's that *!%-#!6*$ Murphy who's got it. No matter, I aim to get it back. Every damn one of 'em was at the cookout last night and somebody sent his boys out there to cut that crop knowing darn good and well that we wouldn't be there at all. I'll kill 'em! I've spent 30 years doin' this county's dirty work for wages less than you'd pay a mule. I ain't goin' to see my retirement money go in some other S.O.B.'s pocket. I figure $200,000 of that is mine. I'm goin' to get it back, or some poor fool's goin' to pay the price!"

Earl Cooper's words reverberated in his head as he sank deeper into the couch. It was that state trooper, he thought to himself, and they had him wired all along. Cooper pondered his own vincibility as he realized that his empire and everything upon which it had been built was slipping from his grasp. Years of hard work—some of it even honest work—were all for naught. A sense of humiliation that he had never known before seized him with gut-wrenching force. "This is it, boys," he said as he staggered toward the door. "This is it."

Later that week Earl Cooper was dead. He had told a deputy that he was going to investigate a moonshine still said to be located on top of Backbone Ridge. The next day the sheriff's body was found at the bottom of a 120-foot ravine. Most folks think he jumped, some say he fell, still others feel he was killed by "the mob;" a few even believe it wasn't his body that was found. For obvious reasons the case of State v. Cooper was scratched from the docket of the state superior court. Shortly thereafter, the sheriff's widow received $50,000 from the Peace Officer's Widow and Orphan Fund. The Fund was established to aid the survivors of law enforcement officers killed in the line of duty.

DISCUSSION QUESTIONS

1. What are some of the patterns of criminality identified in this case? What social-environmental or "structural" conditions permit the types of criminality that are described in the case?
2. Describe Sheriff Cooper's relationship with the citizens of Deerfield County. What bearing does this relationship have on Cooper's attitude toward corrupt practices? In what way is his relationship with his co-conspirators an inverted form of social bonding?
3. Is there a way of characterizing the relationship between the Deerfield Sheriff's Office and other state-level agencies that explains the Sheriff's hostility toward "outsiders?" What accounts for the prolonged inability of state agents to obtain evidence on Sheriff Cooper's illegal activity?
4. How can we explain the relative success of Trooper Green in resisting Cooper's overtures to engage in crime and corruption?
5. Criminal investigators and most of the citizens of Deerfield County believe that Sheriff Cooper committed suicide. Are there any principles of sociology that can aid our understanding of why the Sheriff took his own life?

SUGGESTED READING
"WE'VE GOT A SERIOUS PROBLEM HERE"

Barker, Thomas
   1977 "Peer Group Support for Police Occupational Deviance." *Criminology*. 15: 353-366.

   This article examines the role that the tolerance and complicity of other officers plays in the promotion of police deviance. Especially important is the discussion of the ways in which deviant peer groups socialize new recruits into the acceptance of corruption, and the methods used to discipline officers who threaten to expose illegal practices.

Dorsey, R. Rita and David J. Giacopassi

> 1987 "Demographic and Work-Related Correlates of Police Officer Cynicism." pp. 173-188 in D.B. Kennedy and R.J. Homant (eds.) *Police and Law Enforcement, Vol. 5.* New York: AMS Press.

> Earl Cooper presumed that selfishness was the driving force in social relations. This study examines the correlates of this attitude and other factors that relate to police cynicism. This research indicates that cynicism is far more organizationally based than it is dependent on race, sex, age and other individual characteristics.

Manning, Peter K. and Lawrence John Redlinger

> 1983 "Invitational Edges." pp. 354-369 in C.B. Klockars (ed.) *Thinking about Police: Contemporary Readings.* New York: McGraw-Hill.

> This article describes the opportunity for police corruption within the arena of narcotics enforcement. The authors compare various aspects of legally regulated versus legally suppressed markets, and identify a number of patterns of corruption within narcotics enforcement.

Niederhoffer, Arthur

> 1985 "Police Cynicism." pp. 208-210 in A. Blumberg and E. Niederhoffer (eds.) *The Ambivalent Force: Perspectives on the Police.* New York: Holt, Rinehart, and Winston.

> According to Niederhoffer, cynicism among police officers is a response to the social circumstances of different stages in the career path of officers. Particularly appropriate for this case is the "aggressive cynic" who is driven by a resentment of the conditions of police work. Several hypotheses are generated by Niederhoffer that provide an interesting contrast to the events described in "We've Cot a Serious Problem Here."

Sherman, Lawrence

> 1980. "Three Models of Organizational Corruption in Agencies of Social Control." *Social Problems.* 27: 478-491.

> How do entire law enforcement agencies such as the Deerfield County Sheriff's Department succumb to corruption? Sherman addresses this question by identifying three sets of contingencies under which whole departments can become engrossed in illegal practices. The model of the "internal exploiters" is particularly relevant for the analysis of corrupt law enforcement in Deerfield County.

PART TWO
Criminal Courts

Introduction

Criminal courts constitute the second major segment of the criminal justice system. Comprised of both major trial courts and limited and specialized tribunals, these courts play a pivotal role in criminal law because it is here where the formal issue of legal guilt is determined. Although some have argued that even law enforcement actions can carry punitive consequences, no one would argue about the potentially punitive connotations of court processes.

Like law enforcement, criminal courts are characterized by considerable discretion. Unlike law enforcement, much of the discretionary authority that is exercised therein has not received much attention in either the popular or academic press. With the exception of criminal sentencing which still captures the public and scholarly imagination, the discretionary authority exercised by criminal court personnel largely escapes notice.

The cases included in this section all touch on some aspect of this discretionary authority. The first, *But He's Only a Kid,* focuses on a child who kills his school principal. Faced with a juvenile crime of such magnitude, the district attorney wants to try the child as an adult, something that the state's criminal code permits for children 13 and older. The judge is faced with the prosecutor's motion for an adult trial. As the reader learns more about the case and the judge's dilemma, he/she is forced to look not only at the power inherent in the prosecutorial and judicial functions, but also at the purpose of criminal law and the relationship between the juvenile and adult systems.

Recently, criminal courts have been charged with a lack of sensitivity to black-on-black crime. This surfaces in specific complaints that black offenders who victimize whites are treated more punitively than other offenders and in more general complaints that black-on-black offenses are routinely ignored or downplayed. *Granny With a Gun* deals with the latter with the added complication of age. Specifically, the case tells the story of an elderly widow who kills two teenagers. As the reader learns more about the prosecutor's dilemma, he/she is confronted with the claims of self-defense and the plight of many victims and offenders in contemporary society.

Although the majority of criminal cases are disposed of prior to trial in either guilty pleas or negotiated guilty pleas, criminal trials still capture the public's attention. In the process, the adversarial process that underlies contemporary trial proceedings has received considerable scrutiny. Nowhere is this more evident than in the drama and tension that frequently surround rape trials. *I Was Too Much of a Man for Her* tells the story of one rape trial and draws the reader's attention to the rape shield reforms enacted by almost every state in the 1970s and 1980s. As the reader learns more about the defendant in this rape trial, he/she is also confronted with variations on the crime of rape and on the more general issue of the attorney-client relationship.

More typical than criminal trials is the process of plea bargaining in which a defendant agrees to plead guilty in exchange for a different or lesser charge or for a recommendation for sentence leniency. *Plea Bargaining Ain't So Bad* takes a look at this process against the backdrop of a violent crime. In the case, the reader learns about two defendants who were both involved in a brutal crime. One of the defendants pleads guilty, while the other goes to trial. Examining the differences for both the defendant and the victim, the reader is asked to evaluate the appropriateness of plea bargaining, to assess the cost of criminal trials, and to explain and/or justify the way each of the defendants was treated.

Although the majority of criminal cases are probably not appealed, the image of endless proceedings is fixed on a substantial portion of the public's consciousness. One arena where this image holds true is in the area of capital punishment where the system operates in a deliberately slow and tortuous fashion. *I'm Really Torn* looks at a particular criminal appeal, although the story directs more attention to issues of legal ethics than to either due process or capital punishment. In the case a lawyer is confronted with the fact that his client has lied and that an innocent man has been sentenced to death. The reader is asked to draw a specific appraisal of the lawyer's behavior and to look more generally at the application of capital punishment in our system.

The five cases included in this section touch on issues of considerable import to criminal courts. These range from the basic and routine exercise of discretion to the more convoluted question of legal ethics. In the process, the cases illustrate a number of issues that confront and challenge criminal courts. Here we deal with the specific excuse of self-defense and the effectiveness of shield provisions designed to restrict the adversarial process, as well as the consequences and appropriateness of plea bargaining. The following chart outlines these cases and the concepts and issues that are highlighted in each. Once again, the authors trust that students will offer their own examples and that they will pay attention to comparable cases that have drawn local interest or sparked similar controversy.

PART TWO: Criminal Courts

Case Title	Central Subject	Concepts/Issues
But He's Only a Kid	juvenile crime	prosecutorial and judicial discretion juvenile crime and liability purposes of the criminal sanction
Granny With a Gun	black on black crime	self-defense prosecutorial discretion plight of elderly
I Was Too Much of a Man for Her	rape trial	rape laws including shield provisions types of rape (e.g. date) criminal trial process
Plea Bargaining Ain't So Bad	violent crime	violent crime plea bargaining versus criminal trial consequences of victimization sentencing disparities
I'm Really Torn	criminal appeal	lawyer-client relationship legal ethics capital punishment felony murder

Case Six

But He's Only a Kid

TUESDAY, FEBRUARY 10

Walter McLoughlin, principal of the Southeast Middle School, was having one of his more typical workdays: several lengthy telephone conversations with the superintendent of schools on budgetary issues, a review of the proposed curricular changes in language arts, interviews with two candidates for a seventh grade teaching position, and several parent conferences. The last item, however, was somewhat troubling. One of the parents, Wilma Robinson, had been rather truculent. Her thirteen-year-old son, George, had been disciplined a few days earlier—last Friday to be exact—for one of his more usual violations of school regulations. Discipline in George's case meant paddling. Although Principal McLoughlin was loath to paddle students, occasionally he found it was the only method of discipline he could employ. George's mother was especially disturbed at the paddling. In fact, she seemed to come pretty close to taking a slug at Principal McLoughlin, though her primary expression of frustration and rage was verbal. Describing the injury Principal McLoughlin inflicted on her son, she yelled and screamed about those who were out to "hurt him" and those who, as she put it, "didn't understand that her George had a troubled time, a very troubled time with school."

When Principal McLoughlin called George Gentry into his office the previous Friday, the administrator knew he was going to take the most severe form of discipline possible. George had repeatedly violated a host of school regulations. A seventh grader, he was constantly pushing and hitting other children and generally disruptive in the classroom. Teachers were loath to do anything that even appeared to aggravate him as he had the reputation of being easily frustrated. He also had a reputation for being nasty. In the first grade, he had brought razor blades into the classrooms, necessary, as he put it, "to stop from gittin' hurt." Where he got the blades from or why they were not taken away from him at home were questions teachers didn't bother to ask. They simply tried to keep away and to keep George quiet. It wasn't easy to keep George quiet, though. He would flare up at the slightest provocation, frequently in ways that startled his classmates—all of whom were the same chronological age but far less "street smart."

The "flare-up" that precipitated this trip to Principal McLoughlin's office centered on George's repeated pushing and hitting—specifically, the fact that no one in his classroom would sit near him in language arts or any other class activity. Principal McLoughlin had tried a number of disciplinary measures: he had George stay after school; he tried punitive exercises (difficult, as George couldn't read or write very well); and he sent regular messages home asking for his mother's and, eventually, his father's cooperation. When these measures brought no result, when George continued to "flare up" against his classmates, Principal McLoughlin felt he had no alternative. Sending for one teacher and asking his secretary to observe, he administered the customary five paddles on George's bottom. George murmured something about "ain't fair," but generally was quiet during the proceedings. Neither the teacher or secretary observed any permanent injury. In fact, both agreed that the paddling wasn't severe.

George told his mother about the paddling, and indicated he had taken a substantial beating. Showing his mother bruises on his arm and thigh, he complained that the principal "had it in for him"and wasn't going to let up. In fact, George complained, no one seemed to like him. George's mother didn't offer much reassurance, other than to comment that "everybody is after us, boy—everybody—don't ever shut your eyes on no one 'cause they just out to get you!" She did, however, promise George that she would stop by Principal McLoughlin's office to talk about the paddling.

WEDNESDAY, FEBRUARY 11

Wilma Robinson returned to Principal McLoughlin's office on Wednesday. Since she found little comfort in her Tuesday visit, she brought George along with her. Although she had no precise agenda or issues for discussion, she wanted George to tell Principal McLoughlin his side of the story about the paddling and about his trouble with school. Moreover, she wanted George to show Principal McLoughlin the bruises that still marked his arm and thigh.

Principal McLoughlin wasn't happy to see either Wilma or George. In fact, as he said to his secretary before closing his office door, he wasn't interested in seeing either of them anytime soon. As the conference with Principal McLoughlin continued, the discussion turned into a verbal slugfest. Whether by design or accident, the office door moved ajar and McLoughlin's secretary heard everything. Wilma Robinson yelled and screamed at McLoughlin. She insisted that he was out to get her and her son, that he had been physically abusive, and that he had no business being a school principal. For his part, McLoughlin was no less complimentary. He told Wilma that she wasn't a very fit mother, that her son had a host of problems and was going to land in jail, and that the school couldn't do much with him. During their conversation, McLoughlin asked his secretary to send for the sheriff.

At some point in the discussion, young George reached into his jacket and pulled out a medium-sized kitchen knife. Moving quickly to his mother's side, he lunged at McLoughlin's chest. Stabbing him four times, George finally pushed his mother aside and ran out the door. Wilma Robinson was startled. When George started to stab the principal, she sat back in horror and didn't say anything. But she didn't move to stop him either. McLoughlin's secretary rushed into the room after George ran out and noticed that McLoughlin was on the floor. She called an ambulance and then the sheriff. She didn't have long to wait. The ambulance arrived within minutes and a sheriff's deputy was already in the school building, called in earlier during McLoughlin's discussion with Wilma and her son.

THURSDAY, FEBRUARY 12

Early Thursday morning, Walter McLoughlin died. Emergency surgery was not able to stop the damage wrought by the four stab wounds. He had sustained injuries too deep and lost too much blood to recover. Even prior to McLoughlin's death, the sheriff was out looking for George. He didn't have to look far. George' father, Sam Gentry, brought him in. After the attack, Mrs. Robinson had called George's father and asked him to help her find the boy. Driving all over Carroll County, he found George wandering down a dirt road. Taking the boy with him, he drove to the sheriff's office. The sheriff took George and his father to the local youth detention facility and called the district attorney. The DA indicated that he would approach the Superior Court judge who normally handled adult cases about George. Specifically, he would ask the judge to approve a transfer from juvenile to adult court. Judge Banks had such authority as he presided over juvenile and adult proceedings in Carroll County. There was no separate juvenile court and not enough cases to warrant even the appointment of a part-time juvenile judge.

FRIDAY, FEBRUARY 13

The morning newspaper shouted the headline: "13-year-old apprehended for murder of school principal." The reporter went on to describe the homicide, the boy's "capture" by his father, and his current custody in the youth detention center. She then went on to review the state's juvenile court procedures and the youthful offender provisions. Explaining that George was too young to fall into the youthful offender category (18), she noted that Judge Banks served as both juvenile and adult judge in the county. She also noted that he would hold hearings on the place of George's prosecution the following week.

SATURDAY, FEBRUARY 14

The arrest of the Gentry boy caused quite a stir in the county. Since the youngster was black and the victim white, the local NAACP chapter was concerned about the possibility of adult prosecution. For his part, the DA was no less emphatic, though he took an obviously different posture. "If kids can kill, they should be tried as adults." Furthermore, the DA pointed out that under the state's juvenile court code, young George could only be confined for a maximum of 18 months—insufficient incarceration, the DA insisted—for such a dangerous kid.

The local newspaper again covered several aspects of the case and reviewed pertinent sections of the juvenile code. Local citizens were interviewed—many of whom argued that Judge Banks had to try him as an adult. Although a few citizens argued that "he's only a kid," the murder of a school principal didn't seem to constitute an issue of juvenile justice.

WEDNESDAY, FEBRUARY 18

In an unusual evening proceeding, Judge Banks listened to attorneys arguing in behalf of and against young George Gentry. George's attorney, Kimberly Chilton, emphasized that he was only thirteen, that he had a troubled childhood, and that he deserved a chance to be rehabilitated. Calling a few social workers and NAACP representatives to the stand, Chilton asked the court to try young Gentry as a juvenile. "Only then," Chilton reasoned, "is there any hope of reform. Put him with adult felons and he'll kill some more when he comes out."

The District Attorney took a different position and asked if anyone in the court would like to take young Gentry into his/her home. If not that, he argued, "how about his sitting next to your kid in school?" Few in the courtroom failed to react to that as even the witnesses who spoke in Gentry's behalf did not offer to serve as foster parents. No one in the courtroom seemed to respond positively to the thought of his/her child as young Gentry's classmate. "We have no place for kids like young George," the DA argued. "The juvenile system is not equipped to handle him. It would be nice if it could but wishing won't make rehabilitation a reality. Let's cut our losses with young Gentry now and keep him from hurting others for as long as we can."

EPILOGUE

Judge Banks ruled that George Gentry would be tried as an adult. The date of his trial is still pending and he remains in custody at the youth detention center.

DISCUSSION QUESTIONS

1. Should George Gentry be tried as a juvenile or an adult?
2. To what extent is George's mother (and father) responsible for his actions?
3. Did Principal McLoughlin exacerbate young Gentry's problems at school?
4. What purpose(s) would be served by trying George Gentry as an adult? As a juvenile? How do these purposes conform to ascribed notions of criminal law?
5. Would you like to defend or prosecute George Gentry? Assuming he is tried as an adult, should the state seek the death penalty? Assuming he is tried as a juvenile, what treatment/response would you recommend?
6. How does this case illustrate the limitations of criminal law?

SUGGESTED READING
"BUT HE'S ONLY A KID"

Baker, Keith and Robert J. Rubel

1980 *Violence and Crime in the Schools.* Lexington, Massachusetts: D. C. Heath.

Focusing on school crime and violence, the articles in this book focus on four major issues or themes. These include the extensiveness of troublesome behavior, the school as victim, the responsibility of schools for criminal behavior, and vandalism.

Children's Defense Fund

1976 *Children in Adult Jails.* Washington, D.C.: Children's Defense Fund of the Washington Research Project.

A concise and critical summary of adolescents in the nations adult jails with particular attention to the living conditions therein. The Defense Fund calls for specific reforms at the federal and state levels of government.

Gardiner, Muriel

1976 *The Deadly Innocents: Portraits of Children Who Kill.* New York: Basic Books.

Case studies of youths who have murdered others with particular attention to psychological interpretations or assessments and related background characteristics. Gardiner also speaks to the treatment of youthful offenders in correctional institutions and community-based programs.

Hirschi, Travis

1969 *Causes of Delinquency.* Berkeley, California: University of California Press.

One of the leading arguments on the relevance of social control theory to juvenile delinquency. Hirschi argues that juvenile delinquents do not have the beliefs and expectations that keep most of society in lawful behavior.

Platt, Anthony M.

1969 *The Child Savers.* Chicago: University of Chicago Press.

The analysis of the history of the juvenile justice system with particular emphasis on the 19th Century "child saving" reform movement. Platt offers a critical view of both 19th and 20th Century efforts and argues that neither developments can be considered benign.

Case Seven

Granny With a Gun

FEBRUARY 9, 1986

The Sunday newspapers virtually shouted the story "Gunning Granny Kills Two Youths" Below, the story spelled out the details. A 76-year-old grandmother shot two youths, one 15, the other 17, with a shotgun. A third youth, aged 16, managed to survive with no wounds. As the story went, the "gunning granny" had complained of continual harassment from neighborhood youths over a couple of years. The story briefly hinted at minor physical abuse and verbal intimidation, although the surviving youth argued that they simply liked to "tease" granny. The youth, one Maurice Johnson, said that they were granny's friends, visited her often to "play with her," and were shot at when she "got crazy" one Saturday afternoon.

In addition to describing the crime, the newspaper reporter added a paragraph on pertinent state law. Specifically, she quoted from the penal code's section on justifiable use of deadly force and emphasized that "...a person is justified in threatening or using force against another when and to the extent that he reasonably believes that such threat or force is necessary to prevent or terminate such other's unlawful entry into or attack upon a habitation."

FEBRUARY 10, 1986

On a rainy Monday morning, the district attorney, Barry Felton, nursed a cup of coffee and talked to no one in particular: " What the hell am I going to do with her?" His assistant, Ed Thurmond, knocked gently on the door and asked if he wanted to talk about a burglary case scheduled for court later that week. Felton replied that he was more interested in talking about "granny with a gun," as the newspapers had dubbed Sarah Burns. "Tell me, Thurmond, what are we going to do with her? The press had a field day with this thing and they aren't going to let up. It's absolutely loaded with trouble. The police say the surviving kid insists they were not breaking in, didn't even

45

give the appearance of such. Furthermore, Sarah Burns has a reputation for being difficult, especially with neighborhood kids. The whole thing gets even 'messier' with the fact that it's a black-on-black crime. We're getting a lot of heat for not taking these crimes seriously and we could get into deep trouble if we pretend to ignore this. The 'gray panthers' could also easily raise a ruckus if they think we're closing our eyes to the harassment that senior citizens have complained of in that neighborhood for years. We don't stand to win anything on this one."

APRIL 1, 1985

Sarah Burns sat in the police office nearest her neighborhood, a declining if not dead area of town in a large coastal city. Sarah was known to the officers in the precinct as she had visited repeatedly over a twelve-month period to complain about "vandals and hoods" in the neighborhood. Although she did not file any formal complaints and did not offer any evidence of victimization, she was obviously upset.

"These kids are just hoodlums," Sarah repeated to the desk officer. "They don't respect your property and are always trying to milk you out of the few pennies you have. They don't let you walk down the street without a grab for your purse and lounge around like lizards on 'check day.' Can't you do something about them?"

The desk officer, Sergeant Mitchell, listened patiently to Mrs. Burns, but knew that nothing would come of the conversation. Since Sarah offered no specific complaint, there was nothing he could do but promise that the police would try to patrol the area, a promise that he knew was somewhat shallow since the force could not guarantee "round-the-clock" protection for any citizen. He was, though, sympathetic to Mrs. Burns, despite the fact that other officers regarded her as something of a crank. The neighborhood she lived in —popularly known as Panic Village—was tough, very tough indeed. Kids did prowl around and they did haunt the "old folks," especially on "check day" when welfare and social security checks were generally received. Although many in the neighborhood were advised to have their checks deposited directly in bank accounts, many of the seniors didn't trust "banks" and persisted in cashing their checks shortly after reception. In this instance, Mrs. Burns was a bit of an exception. Though she held onto her social security check, she waited a week or so after the first in the naive hope that potential muggers would leave her alone later in the month. In that she was likely to be sadly mistaken. Word got around pretty quickly that ole Burns held onto her check longer than most.

FEBRUARY 8, 1986

Saturday was a dreary day. The rain kept coming and the sky seemed dark for the better part of both morning and afternoon. The day before Sarah Burns had walked to the nearest bank and cashed her modest social security check, money she received for years of work as a hospital cleaning lady. As she walked home from the bank she was followed by several teenagers who taunted her with jokes and not-so-veiled threats. "Why don't you come play with us,"one yelled. "How about some money for candy," another hollered. "Ooooo, wouldn't you just love to get your hands on some of momma's dough," still another shouted. One youth, a teenager named Maurice Johnson, grabbed Sarah Burns' arm and pleaded for a few bucks: "Just somethin' to git some food," he emphasized. Sarah Burns wanted to ignore the remarks, but she kept telling the teenagers, about five or six young men aged 13 to 17 years, that she wished the police would round them all up and put them away.

The afternoon of February 8, three teenaged boys approached Sarah Burns's house and pounded on the front door. Sarah's home was a row house with a small front porch. It virtually touched similar structures on both sides. Fading curtains hung from the two front windows from which Sarah could view the street scene below. Most of the time, Sarah ignored any knocks on her doors. Many of her old friends had died. Some fortunate few had moved away. Getting more accustomed to the life of a recluse, she had spoken to few people in the past few years. In fact, most of the conversations she had, other than her brief and pointed response to the neighborhood youth, were with the local police. When she heard the pounding on the front door, Sarah did as usual; she looked out and didn't move. The three youths, Maurice Johnson, Walton Jones, and Sam Goodfellow, saw Mrs. Burns peek out around the front window curtains. Seeing that, they pounded even louder. Though neither Sarah or Maurice could remember how long, police estimated that the three were on the porch for at least five minutes.

The rest of the story, however, was not disputed. As the pounding grew louder, the front door opened. Sarah stood there with her deceased husband's shotgun and threatened the youths. "Go away or I'll shoot," she cried. "Oh, granny," Maurice responded, "you ain't goin' shoot us. We just want to talk." At that, Mrs. Burns fired several shots at the youths, hitting Jones and Goodfellow, but missing Johnson. Jones and Goodfellow lost consciousness immediately. Emergency surgery at the nearest hospital wasn't successful, however, and they both died late Saturday evening. Maurice Johnson lived and kept crying, "She's crazy, she's crazy."

FEBRUARY 11, 1986

Barry Felton and Ed Thurmond were talking about the Burns case. Looking over the police report, they were obviously distraught. There's no question that Sarah Burns killed the two youths. There's also no evidence that the three were doing anything illegal. Knowing the neighborhood and having the police department's summary of Sarah Burns, long-standing complaints, however, they were sympathetic. "We can't give the black community the impression that we're ignoring black-on-black crime, and homicide is as serious as you can get," Thurmond said. "We're also apt to have the civil liberties types coming on as crime control nuts if we don't move quickly on this. But tell me, what are the old people in Panic Village going to do? What relief can we promise them?"

EPILOGUE

The DA did pursue the case of <u>People v. Sarah Burns,</u> albeit with some reluctance. During the trial, the local public defender argued in Sarah's behalf and built a claim of self-defense. Emphasizing that Sarah was a prisoner in her own home, he brought in several witnesses who supported her claim that neighborhood youths were constantly harassing older folks and milking them of their few pennies. Sarah's attorney then called in several expert witnesses who testified about the nature of fear, physiological and rational responses to fear, and perceptions about threats. Although the state tried to point out that Sarah's action did not constitute a reasonable response to real fear, the DA did not press the point and, at times, seemed to be siding with the defense. In the final analysis, the jury acquitted Sarah Burns of the homicide charges. She was, however, found guilty of a technical firearms violation. The judge has yet to set sentence.

DISCUSSION QUESTIONS

1. Should Sarah Burns be prosecuted? If so, for what offense? If not, why?
2. Would you want to defend Sarah Burns if she were charged with a criminal offense? Why?
3. Were the prosecutors really on the horns of a dilemma with the "granny with a gun?"
4. What justification and/or excuses could be raised in Saran Burns's defense?
5. Should victim vulnerability enter into the seriousness with which we consider some crimes?
6. How does the case of Sarah Burns compare to that of the New York subway vigilante, Bernhard Goetz?

SUGGESTED READING
"GRANNY WITH A GUN"

Cole, George F.
   1970   "The Decision to Prosecute." *Law and Society Review*
   4:313-343.
   The classic analysis of prosecutorial discretion with particular emphasis on the appropriateness of an exchange model of clientele relationships.

Fletcher, George
   1970   *Rethinking Criminal Law.* Boston: Little, Brown.
   An exhaustive reconsideration of the basic principles and concepts of criminal law. Chapter Ten on justifications and excuses offers a provocative analysis of related theories and their practical applications.

Katz, Leo

1987 *Bad Acts and Guilty Minds: Conundrums of the Criminal Law*. Chicago: University of Chicago Press.

A provocative and playful analysis of the central elements of criminal liability. Drawing on a variety of disciplines, Katz offers a series of interesting discussions on criminal intent, the criminal act, and related justifications and excuses.

Rubin, Lilian S.

1986 *Quiet Rage: Bernie Goetz in a Time of Madness*. Berkeley, California: University of California Press.

A psychological and social analysis of the case of Bernhard Goetz, the so-called "subway vigilante" who relied on self defense in the shooting of four black teenagers on a New York City subway. Rubin does not offer an extensive analysis of self defense, but dwells on the background of the defendant and his four victims.

Stanko, Elizabeth Anne

1981-82 "The Impact of Victim Assessment on Prosecutors' Screening Decisions: The Case of the New York County District Attorney's Office." *Law and Society Review* 16: 225-238.

An analysis of the effect of victim characteristics in prosecutorial decision making. Stanko found evidence of substantial partiality and argued that victim credibility played an important role in the decision to prosecute.

Case Eight

I was Too Much of a Man for Her

THE INCIDENT

On Friday evening, May 6, police at the Hanover Precinct Station responded to a call from the night clerk at the Sunset Motor Inn that a rape had taken place in the vicinity of the motel. When the police arrived at the scene they discovered that the alleged victim was a black female, approximately twenty years old, who was clothed only in a blanket that had been given to her by the motel clerk. According to the victim, her assailant was a black male known to her as "Handsome Ray." She stated that she was assaulted at gunpoint in a weed-infested vacant lot adjacent to The Reggae Lounge, a popular juke joint that was about one block from the motel. According to the statement given to the officer at the scene, the suspect ordered the woman to undress after which she was thrown into a clump of bushes where she was raped and sodomized (i.e., forced to submit to anal intercourse). Later in the evening after gathering corroborative information from patrons of the Reggae Lounge, police officers arrested Rayford Hopkins, a 19-year-old black male from the Hanover neighborhood, who was a regular at the lounge. Upon booking, Hopkins was charged with first degree sexual assault and aggravated sodomy.

THE VICTIM

The victim, Venita Jones, was a young woman with a bad reputation in the community. Seventeen years old and unmarried, she was already the mother of two small children fathered by different men. Within the community she was generally regarded as a town "tramp", indifferent to the welfare of her children, a regular at local gathering spots and social clubs, and reputed to be an "easy" woman. Interpersonally, she was perceived as sullen and inarticulate. Although she was receptive to sleazy overtures from men, she was also known to have a vituperous and quick temper. She conceded to knowing the defendant, but vehemently denied having either dated or engaged in sexual relations with him previous to the incident on May 6.

On the night of the alleged assault, she had gone out to "play" at the Reggae. According to her statement to the police, she had left the bar at about 11:15 p.m. She claimed that the defendant had followed her out of the building and overtook her as she cut across a vacant lot on her way home. It was at this location that he forced her, at gunpoint, to submit to having sex with him. After he had assaulted her, Venita Jones was able to run to the lobby of the nearby motel and have the desk clerk call the police.

Physical evidence taken from the victim indicated that she had had sexual relations shortly before the examination and that she had multiple scrapes and scratches that were not inconsistent with injuries that might have been sustained from a sexual assault in an area filled with bushes and bramble. There was no additional evidence that the victim had been beaten or physically assaulted (other than the evidence indicating possible sexual assault).

THE DEFENDANT

The alleged assailant, Rayford Hopkins, had a community-wide reputation as a lady's man. Well-built and exceedingly handsome, the 19-year-old Hopkins was the epitome of the stereotypical "macho dude." His version of the incident outside of the Reggae was quite different from that of Venita Jones. According to Hopkins, Jones and he had dated previously and on several of those occasions engaged in sexual relations. He claimed that the incident occurred when he encountered Jones on the street outside the club where she agreed to slip into the bushes with him to have sex. After they had uncoupled, he claims that an argument ensued over his involvement with other women. According to Hopkins, Jones ran naked to the motel enraged with jealousy and driven by the intention of embarrassing him. Hopkins argued that he could not have raped her at gunpoint because he was not carrying a gun at the time of the incident. More pointedly, Hopkins vehemently denied raping Jones because he did not "need" to rape a woman in order to satisfy himself sexually.

THE CLIENT-ATTORNEY RELATIONSHIP

Teresa Wilson had many years of experience in the public defender's office. She realized that for a variety of reasons Hopkins' defense would be difficult; still, she felt that in this case there was a good chance that Hopkins could be acquitted. In walking the thin line between casting the case in its best light for the defense and "trying the victim," Wilson understood that the strategy to be employed at Hopkins' trial would need to be carefully crafted. There would be no point, for instance, in arguing that

Hopkins had not had intercourse with Jones; this was a fact acknowledged by everyone involved in the case. There was at least some chance, perhaps enough to convince a jury, that the incident outside the Reggae had indeed been consensual. How this could be presented in court was the essential problem in Hopkins' defense.

The greatest liability the defense faced in this case was the nature of the criminal charges against Hopkins. Allegations involving sex crimes always provide the prosecution with fertile ground upon which to appeal to the sympathy of jurors. One of the main strategies for defending clients charged with other types of personal crime, an examination of the degree to which the incident was victim precipitated, was typically closed off in sex crime cases.

In this particular case, there were three especially damaging pieces of evidence to contend with: (1) the irrefutable evidence that Ms. Jones had had sexual relations; (2) the cuts and scratches she had received in the bushes where the incident took place; and (3) the fact that she had run naked to the motel to report the alleged attack. In regard to this later aspect of the case, any interpretation of Ms. Jones's behavior other than one consistent with rape victimization, would have made her actions seem utterly bizarre.

The factors operating on Hopkins' behalf were substantial and important, but required the highest degree of caution in how they would be introduced into evidence. The experience of Teresa Wilson suggested to her that Rayford Hopkins might very well be innocent. Work in the public defender's office often involved dealing with uncertainty in regard to a defendant's guilt or innocence. Candor was not the greatest asset of the ordinary criminal defendant; all too often defendants would lie to their own attorney. In Hopkins' case, Wilson was convinced that the outcome of the trial would turn on whether the jury chose to believe Hopkins or Venita Jones.

The gun that Hopkins used in the alleged assault had never been found. A man who had claimed to have seen Hopkins carrying the gun at the Reggae the night of the incident had also been involved in an altercation with Hopkins the same night. His testimony could be discredited. Venita Jones, for her part, would not be a particularly persuasive prosecution witness. In spite of her youth and desperate circumstances, Jones offered the strongest profile of a street-wise, cynical, hard woman. Her presentation of self would not elicit much sympathy. Furthermore, Rayford Hopkins insisted that he and the alleged victim had had a prior relationship that included sexual intimacy. If this were indeed true, it was entirely plausible that the episode outside the Reggae was no more than a sexual liaison that had gone sour.

In Wilson's mind there was certainly enough legitimate doubt regarding what had actually happened to sustain an acquittal for her client. How to successfully introduce this information into evidence was the problem. A direct frontal assault on the moral character of Venita Jones was out of the question. If Wilson decided to impugn the character of Jones, she was required to produce corroborative evidence to sustain her accusations; to do otherwise was to risk inflaming the jury (which might occur anyway) and to invite a contempt of court citation from the trial judge. The strategy would have to be developed with Rayford Hopkins' cooperation; he would have to testify to his previous relationship with Ms. Jones.

Having Hopkins testify was not without risk. Obviously, if he took the stand in his own defense, he would be exposed to cross-examination by the prosecution. This alone, however, was not a big problem since Hopkins had no prior record of involvement in violent crime and there was little else in his background that would have been a source of embarrassment. The trouble was that in his own way, Hopkins had a personality that was every bit as obnoxious as Venita Jones's. To say that Hopkins was infatuated by his own sexual prowess was an understatement. Haughty, self-absorbed, condescending in his attitude toward women, and especially arrogant, these were all apt descriptions of Hopkins' demeanor. Teresa Wilson was troubled by Hopkins' persistent claim that sexual assault was, for him, a behavioral impossibility. He had informed her repeatedly that he didn't "need" to rape women to achieve sexual gratification. Hopkins perceived the charges against him not as unjust or wrong, but rather as an affront to his dignity. This he could not suffer lightly. In his mind, his innocence was clearly established by his reputation as a sexual giant, a complete and sufficient defense. He viewed the charges against him with absolute contempt.

Wilson realized full well that if even a hint of Hopkins' arrogance saw the light of day during his trial, the case would be lost. As the trial date approached, she once again reviewed each of her strategic options. First, she could decide ahead of time not to risk having Hopkins take the stand. If this strategy were pursued, she would hope that the physical evidence would do minimum damage to her case and that Venita Jones would not be successfully cast as a sympathetic victim. Second, Ms. Wilson could wait to see if Jones's reputation were vulnerable, in which case she would call Hopkins to the stand in the hope that his testimony would add further damaging evidence to the prosecution's case, and that Hopkins would not, at the same time, alienate the jury. Third, Wilson could attempt to make the creditability of Jones as a rape victim the central issue at trial. If this strategy were pursued, Hopkins would have to testify to his alleged prior relationship with Jones while not defining himself as an egotistical jerk. The third option was the most attractive if Hopkins behaved himself on the stand. Given her seeming inability to get through to him about his attitude, Wilson could not be sure that Hopkins would serve his own self-interest during his trial.

THE TRIAL

The district attorney had already called a number of witnesses to testify in the case against Rayford Hopkins: the arresting police officer, the motel clerk, and a physician who presented the medical evidence from the rape examination of Venita Jones. When it became Ms. Jones's turn to testify there was little in the district attorney's line of questioning that yielded new or unexpected information. From Teresa Wilson's viewpoint, Ms. Jones's flat, unemotional, and seemingly rehearsed performance was uncharacteristic of the type of testimony that was most likely to win sympathy from a jury. Wilson realized that this was her opportunity to discredit Jones as a reliable witness. State law and legal ethics dictated, however, that any attempt to discredit the testimony of Venita Jones could not involve a direct attack on her moral character. The rape shield laws of the state specifically forbade defense attorneys from inquiring into an alleged rape victim's sexual behavior with anyone other than the defendant. Even an allegation of prior sexual involvement with a defendant could not be pursued without corroborative evidence.

Teresa Wilson decided that her cross-examination of Venita Jones would attempt to establish three points: (1) she would seek to indirectly show that Jones was no paragon of virtue; (2) that Jones and Hopkins were from the same neighborhood and knew each other socially; and (3), that Jones and Hopkins had dated and, in fact, were previously involved in an intimate relationship. If she were successful at each of these junctures, Wilson would be required to call Rayford Hopkins to the stand, but little would be needed from him other than a corroborative statement that he and Jones had been sexually involved prior to the alleged incident outside of the Reggae Lounge. Wilson felt that if these points were established she would have done a good job of creating reasonable doubt regarding the validity of the rape charge. If the jury believed that the encounter between Jones and Hopkins may have been consensual, then there was a chance that her client would be acquitted.

Wilson began her cross-examination with a series of innocuous questions designed to set the witness at ease. Afterward, she initiated her more pertinent line of questioning.

"Ms. Jones, is it true that you live at 2731 K Street, Apt. C?"

"That's right," Venita Jones replied.

"Is it true that you live with your mother, and your two children, Shawnda, age 2, and Robert, age 10 months?" asked Wilson in a neutral tone.

"Yea," Jones answered as if bored by the question.

"And you were 17 years old on your last birthday?"

"So?" Jones responded with sudden defensiveness.

Wilson chided Jones with studied patience. "Please, just answer the question."

"Yea, I'm seventeen."

Wilson continued. "Ms. Jones, in your earlier testimony you stated that you were at the Reggae Lounge for about two to three hours on the night that Mr. Hopkins allegedly attacked you. Is that correct?"

"That's about right," answered Jones.

"Does the Reggae Lounge serve alcoholic beverages?"

"I guess they do."

"Ms. Jones, on the night in question, did you drink any alcohol during the time that you were inside the Reggae?" Teresa Wilson inquired pointedly.

Jones responded bluntly. "No."

Wilson shot back incredulously, "You are saying that you were there two or three hours partying and you drank no liquor?"

"Yea, that's right. You got it."

Wilson paused, framing in her mind the next question. "Would you say that Rayford Hopkins is well known in your neighborhood?"

"Yea, everybody knows who Ray is," Venita Jones replied.

Wilson continued. "Prior to the night in question, did you know Mr. Hopkins personally?"

"I know him."

"Is it true that you have socialized at Rayford Hopkins' apartment.

"Yea, but other people be there too."

Wilson refined her question. "Have you ever been at his home alone when only the two of you were there?"

"No, that ain't never happened," Jones retorted.

"Have you ever dated Rayford Hopkins?" Wilson inquired seemingly ignoring Jones's response to the previous question.

Judge Rupert Akers intervened before Venita Jones could answer. "Hold it. Do not answer that question just yet," he instructed Jones.

Turning toward the jury, Akers addressed them. "The jury will please leave the room so that I may visit with counsel before this line of questions continues. You folks don't get too comfortable, I'm going to call you back in just a minute."

After the jury had left the courtroom, Judge Akers called Teresa Wilson to the bench. "Counselor, are you aware of the content of the rape shield law of this state?"

"Yes, I am, your Honor," Wilson replied.

"So you know then, that if you take this line of questioning in the direction I think you are going, it will be your responsibility to produce independent corroboration of any suspicions you raise about the character of the present witness?"

"Yes, your Honor, I am aware of this. It is my intention to call my client to testify in this regard," Teresa Wilson informed Judge Akers.

"Very well. At the appropriate time, I will have something to say to the defendant before he is called to the stand. I think we are ready to continue."

After the jury had returned to the courtroom, Teresa Wilson continued her cross-examination of Venita Jones. "Ms. Jones we were talking about your acquaintanceship with my client. Is it our understanding that you had visited with Rayford Hopkins at his apartment prior to the incident at the Reggae?"

"Yea, I've been to his place before," replied Jones. Wilson continued. "As I asked you before, is it true that you have dated Mr. Hopkins?"

Jones responded angrily. "Naw, I ain't never dated that dude!" Wilson inquired again, "Is it your testimony that you and Rayford Hopkins have never had a boyfriend-girlfriend relationship."

"No way! Never!" Jones rejoined.

Reluctant to press the issue further, Wilson turned to Judge Akers. "I have no other questions of this witness at this time, your Honor."

Akers glanced in the direction of the district attorney. The district attorney rose promptly and informed the Court: "Your Honor, the State rests its case."

After Venita Jones completed her testimony, Judge Akers again sent the jury out and described to Rayford Hopkins his right to avoid possible self-incrimination. He then called a ten minute recess in order to allow Ms. Wilson time to chat with her client prior to his taking the stand. Wilson still believed that an acquittal of Hopkins was possible, but she was very concerned about his demeanor and what he would say when he took the stand. Throughout the time that the case was being investigated and prepared for trial, Hopkins had repeatedly told Wilson that he was eager to testify in his own behalf, again, his basic argument being that he didn't "need" to rape women to satisfy himself sexually. Wilson realized that the case would immediately be lost if Hopkins expressed this sentiment. During the trial break she once again encouraged him to view the case from a juror's perspective and to try to present himself in a way that would make a favorable impression on the jury.

When the trial resumed, Rayford Hopkins was called to the stand to present his version of what had happened on the night of May 6. Consistent with his earlier story, Hopkins claimed that Venita Jones and he had left the Reggae Lounge together with the mutual prospect that they would find a location where they could engage in sexual relations. According to Hopkins a spot in the bushes in the lot adjacent to the Reggae seemed like an adequate location at the time. Hopkins further testified that an argument had ensued after they had sex and that Jones ran naked to the motel as a way of "getting him."

After permitting him to provide his account of the incident, Wilson questioned Hopkins about his alleged past relationship with Jones. His testimony was consistent with that of Jones up to the point where she had been asked if they had dated. It was now time for Hopkins to be asked the three most important questions he would have to answer.

"Mr. Hopkins," Wilson inquired, "would it be accurate to say that you had dated Ms. Jones prior to May 6?"

"Yea, that would be ACCURATE, all right!" Hopkins conceded smugly.

"On any of these occasions did you and Venita Jones engage in sexual relations?" Wilson asked as clearly and unequivocally as possible.

"Yea, we've talked."

"Excuse me?" countered Wilson.

"Say, you know, we've talked . . . had sex —'got it on,'" he proudly reported.

Wilson followed up quickly. "How many times would you guess that you and Venita Jones had sex prior to May 6?"

Hopkins lapsed into narcissistic self-absorption as he casually dismissed the main point of the question. "Who's counting?" smirked Hopkins. "Too many times to remember."

"My God, what a creep!" Wilson thought to herself as she pondered how far she should go in permitting Hopkins to make a fool of himself. One necessary question remained to be asked.

"Mr. Hopkins, please try to answer my next question as clearly and simply as possible. Perhaps a simple 'yes' or 'no' answer will do. Is it your testimony that Venita Jones voluntarily accompanied you to a location next to the Reggae Lounge on the night of May 6 for the purpose of having sexual intercourse, and that at no time did you use force or the threat of force as a way of imposing your desires on her?"

As Rayford Hopkins prepared to answer Wilson's question he straightened in his chair, raised his chin, and threw a look of contempt and condescension in the direction of Venita Jones. He answered defiantly. "I ain't gotta rape no woman. I got plenty of women, all the women I want. I was just too much of a man for her!"

Teresa Wilson was an experienced trial attorney. She knew that the jury was just as likely to take their cues about the veracity of testimony from the behavior of the contending attorneys as they were from what was said by the witnesses. She matter of factly announced to the court that she had no further questions of Rayford Hopkins. She walked confidently to the defense table, sat down and rearranged some papers on the table. As the district attorney rose to cross-examine Hopkins, Wilson pondered the simplicity of his task. Rayford Hopkins, it seemed, had done the prosecutor's job for him.

DISCUSSION QUESTIONS

1. Do you feel that the facts in this case are typical of alleged rapes? Atypical? Stereotypical?
2. Do you think that the physical evidence in this case is sufficient to convict Rayford Hopkins?
3. Do you think Venita Jones's background should be considered by the jury? How do "rape shield laws" protect the interests of alleged rape victims?
4. What are the basic claims that Rayford Hopkins makes in his own defense? Would a jury take each of these claims seriously? According to Hopkins, what type of a crime is rape?
5. Teresa Wilson was afraid that Rayford Hopkins would ruin his own defense if he testified. Why did she harbor this fear? Do you think he harmed his interests through his testimony?

SUGGESTED READING
"I WAS TOO MUCH OF A MAN FOR HER"

Baron, Larry and Murray A. Straus

   1987 "Four Theories of Rape: A Macrosociological Analysis." *Social Problems*. 34: 467-487.

   The authors formulate an integrated theory of rape built upon four theories that emphasize the cultural and social context of rape. The authors report that social contexts that promote gender inequality and social disorganization have a particularly significant impact on the incidence of rape.

Burt, Martha R.

   1980 "Cultural Myths and Supports for Rape." *Journal of Personality and Social Psychology*. 38: 217-230.

   The "rape myth" that women in various ways invite sexual assault is described. The author then identifies a causal model of factors that influence the acceptance of rape mythology. Specifically, factors such as sex role stereotyping, "adversarial sexual beliefs," and acceptance of interpersonal violence are identified as antecedent to acceptance of rape myths.

LaFree, Gary

   1980 "The Effects of Sexual Stratification by Race on Official Reactions to Rape." *American Sociological Review*. 45: 842-854

   Reactions to allegations of rape have strongly differed historically on the basis of the race of the victim and the race of the offender. LaFree's study demonstrates the tendency in society for reactions to rape to be less severe in intraracial cases of black offender-black victim assaults.

LaFree, Gary, Barbara F. Reskin and Christy A. Visher

   1985 "Jurors' Responses to Victims' Behavior and Legal Issues in Sexual Assault Trials." *Social Problems*. 32: 389-407.

   Sexual assault trials usually involve one of four types of defenses by alleged offenders: that no sex act occurred, consent on the part of the alleged victim, misidentification of the assailant, or a claim of diminished responsibility. The research shows that in cases of alleged consent the victim's behavior receives special scrutiny by jurors regarding especially, drug and alcohol use and any sexual activity outside of marriage.

Scully, Diana and Joseph Marolla

1984.   "Convicted Rapists' Vocabulary of Motive: Excuses and Justifications." *Social Problems*. 31: 530-544.

This study was conducted with a sample of convicted rapists who were asked by the researchers to give accounts for their behavior. The study found that some rapists admitted their offenses while others denied that a rape occurred. Deniers typically resort to "justifications" to explain their behavior, often claiming that the behavior of the victim precipitated the assault. Admitters often invoke "excuses" such as alcohol impairment to account for their behavior.

Thornton, Billy, Michael Robbins, and Joel A. Johnson

1981.   "Social Perception of the Rape Victim's Culpability: The Influence of Respondents' Personal-Environmental Causal Attribution Tendencies." *Human Relations*. 34: 225-237.

Thornton et al. document the different attributional processes that males and females employ in assessing the culpability of female rape victims. Significantly, males were found to assess culpability on the basis of "precipitation-responsibility" to a greater extent than females. Also, males to a greater extent than females based attributions on the personal characteristics of victims.

Case Nine

Plea Bargaining Ain't So Bad

THE CRIME

It was a warm June morning in Madison, a moderate sized city in upstate New York. Jeanne Cardinal listened to the weather report as she packed her girls' lunchboxes for school. As her two daughters came into the kitchen, she observed that it was too hot for either school or her aerobics class. Elizabeth and Emily agreed, although the proximity of the last day of the school year would elicit that response under any weather conditions. After sending the girls off on the school bus, Jeanne took her purse and car keys and drove to the local gym where her aerobics class met every Thursday morning.

Although her class did not start until 9:00 a.m., Jeanne arrived early. She generally liked to be on time so that she didn't have to rush in and join the exercises in progress. Also, it was nice to chat with the other women who attended the class. After, they were usually too tired or busy to stop for conversation. This morning, Jeanne noticed that none of the other women had arrived. "I'm the first one," she said to herself as she pulled up and parked her car. Locking the car door, she proceeded to walk into the building and wait for the other women to arrive. The door was open as the janitor usually arrived before 8:00 a.m. to set things up.

As Jeanne walked into the building, she proceeded down the corridor that led to the main gym where her aerobics class met. The class liked to meet there as they had plenty of room and didn't worry about bumping into other members. There were smaller rooms off the corridor, but these were reserved for those who worked out on exercise machines or for smaller classes. Additionally, there was an equipment room where the janitor stored extra supplies. Heading toward the larger gym, Jeanne was grabbed from behind by a tall man. Just as quickly, another put a hand over her mouth and told her that if she kept quiet nothing would happen.

Panic seized Jeanne, but she maintained enough composure to tell the two men that they could have her purse and car keys. Taking them away, they pushed her into the nearby storage room. One of the men, Sam, took her purse and picked up the car keys that had fallen on the floor. As Sam headed to the door, his partner started to beat Jeanne on the face and the back of the head. "Are you crazy," Sam said. "What's gotten into you. We have to get out of here." As if he didn't hear, Mickey continued the beating. Jeanne tried to ward off the blows and begged the man to stop. Eventually she lost consciousness.

Looking at the severe bruises his partner had inflicted, Sam whispered, "We'd better tie her up so that no one finds her till we're far away." Mickey agreed, and took some rope out of the small closet in the corner of the storage room. "Let's put her in here," he said. Tying her up, Sam cried, "She doesn't seem to be breathing. You killed her, man!" "Who cares," Mickey responded. "Let's just tie her up." After securing her arms and hands, Mickey grabbed the remaining rope and tied it around her neck.

THE AFTERMATH

In what would eventually be calculated as forty-five minutes, Jeanne regained consciousness. Blood poured from her face and head, and she thought she was dying. If only I could get help, she later remembered moaning to herself. Struggling on her knees, she pushed the door of the closet open. Squirming her way to the end of the room, she managed to hit the door of the storage room with her foot. As she did so, one of her class members was exiting the building. Noticing the door and Jeanne's foot, she pulled it open. Screaming, "I think it's Jeanne! Somebody call an ambulance," she ran into the gym.

The class aerobics teacher shouted, "I'll call. You go to her." As the remaining members of the class bent down, another observed, "It's Jeanne, all right. My God, what happened." The ambulance was quick in arriving, primarily because the city's major firehouse was two blocks away. The paramedics attended to Jeanne while one of the other class members said, "I'll call her husband."

At the hospital, Jeanne was rushed into the emergency room where doctors proceeded to clean her face, temporarily stop the flow of blood, and order tests to determine the extent of the injury. Jeanne's husband, Max, arrived and stayed at his wife's side. After hours of tests and numerous stitches, the doctor concluded that, surprisingly, there would be no permanent damage. Although Jeanne suffered a severe concussion, extensive facial bruises, a broken nose, and a harsh rope burn around the neck, she did not exhibit any signs of permanent neurological or structural damage. Max breathed a sigh of relief, although he did wonder about the emotional consequences. The next day, Jeanne was able to give the local police an account of the crime. She described her arrival at the gym, the surprise and beating, and the other details she could remember. Because it was still difficult for her to talk, they didn't press for additional information, nor ask her to examine mug shots. However, they proceeded to interview all of the gym's employees and the members of Jeanne's aerobics class.

Several days later Jeanne was released from the hospital. Her face was still badly swollen, her eyes severely black, and the scabs and stitches quite sore. The police stopped by her home and asked if she could provide any more details about her attackers. Jeanne proceeded to share all that she could and stressed that she was sure that the two were male, white and tall. When asked to look at photos in a police "mug book," Jeanne was able to pick out one of the men. "That's him," she said. "That's the one who hit me," she repeated as she came to Mickey's photo. The police thanked her and assured her that Mickey would soon be in custody.

THE OFFENDERS

After Jeanne blacked out and they had tied her arms, hands, and neck, Sam and Mickey left the building and took Jeanne's car. Although some members of the exercise class had already arrived by then, they were not noticed. It wasn't hard to identify Jeanne's car because the key ring bore the make. Driving out of the park, the pair quickly drove to the entrance to the interstate where they headed southwest. By nightfall they had left New York and were secure, so they thought, in a different state.

As soon as Jeanne had identified one of her attackers, the New York police issued an all-points bulletin for Mickey. Earlier, they had issued a similar call for her car. Within short order, they received word from police officials in Clifton, Pennsylvania, that Mickey had been picked up.

When the police found Mickey, he was alone. Sam had decided to leave, apparently concerned that the two of them would soon be charged with murder. Telling Mickey that he thought he could cut a deal since he had not actually hit the woman, he had decided to return to New York and was planning to turn himself in. Hitching rides back, he walked into a police department in Jackson about 100 miles from Madison and told the startled desk sergeant that he was an accomplice to a homicide.

After taking Sam's confession and getting as many details as they could, the Jackson Police notified their Madison counterparts that they had Mickey's partner in custody. Drawing up both Sam and Mickey's rap sheet, the Madison investigators commented "With rap sheets like this, the violence of the thing and the evidence, the DA should go for the jugular. They should fry." Similar sentiments were voiced by Jeanne's family who were horrified at the extent and senselessness of the crime. "It isn't as if she wouldn't fork over the purse and keys," a cousin remarked, while others were far less restrained.

Sam and Mickey did have extensive rap sheets. Although Sam had not been convicted of a violent offense, he did have some arrests for assault and battery, and a history of burglaries and other minor offenses. Mickey's criminal history was even more pronounced. He had served time for armed robbery and aggravated assault and had a record of property offenses as well. The DA's office charged the two with aggravated assault, armed robbery, and lesser included offenses. "We'll push this one," they assured Jeanne and her husband, Max.

THE PLEA BARGAIN

The case against Sam and Mickey proceeded with considerable dispatch. Since the crime, only two weeks had passed when both were in police custody, and three when the DA filed the charges. Since the offense was unusually brutal for Madison, the case was starting to receive considerable coverage in the local press. The DA wanted to move quickly. "Let's wrap this up while everyone's outraged," he said to one of his assistants. "We've got two losers, an awful crime, and terrific evidence. Trial or not, we can put them away."

Public defenders were assigned to both Sam and Mickey, although Mickey would later ask for a new attorney. Just before trial, Sam decided that he had nothing to gain by letting a court tie him to Mickey. "Hey," he said to his attorney, Marc Goodstein, "I didn't touch her and I told him he was crazy. Could we cut a deal?" Sam's attorney, a rather recent law school graduate, wasn't too unhappy with Sam's request. Although he was excited about the prospect of a trial, he didn't think he had much to gain with this one. Assuring Sam that he would check with the DA, he reminded Sam that he would have to help the DA out if he wanted a fair shake. Sam agreed that he would.

Shortly after talking with Sam, Marc Goodstein walked over to the DA's office and cornered one of the assistants. "My man's ready to help out," he said. "Could you put through a recommendation for a lesser charge or, at worst, a shorter sentence." Bargaining on the charge and sentence was pretty common in the Madison courthouse, so the assistant agreed to check the offer out with his boss.

Anxious to soothe an obviously hurt and frightened victim, the DA's office reviewed the proposed deal with Jeanne and emphasized that they were only willing to negotiate on the sentence. After a lengthy review of the parole system and their expectations about time served, the DA and Jeanne agreed that the state would recommend a sentence of five to nine years. When Goodstein reviewed the terms of the deal with Sam, he emphasized that five to nine wasn't bad. "You'll be out in about three and a half and you could have been stuck with 15 to 20." "Plea bargaining ain't bad, I guess," Sam replied.

THE TRIAL

Mickey's case proceeded to trial. Although Jeanne's facial wounds and injuries had healed by the time the case came up on the calendar (almost six months to the date of the offense), she was still a frightened and vulnerable person. As the trial date approached, Jeanne was apprehensive. To be sure, she didn't have to worry about a conviction. The state's case was airtight: her positive identification, the co-defendant's testimony, and plenty of physical evidence. Mickey was arrested in Jeanne's car, and his fingerprints were lifted from the storage and closet doorknobs at the gym.

Some of her fears were realized at trial where Mickey seemed driven to put on a show. Claiming innocence, he repeated that he had not attacked Jeanne, that they had the wrong guy, and that he intended no harm. That he persisted in these claims in the face of Jeanne's positive identification, Sam's testimony, and the extensive physical evidence was viewed as incredible by most observers. In fact, the judge appeared to lose patience with Mickey's frequent outbursts and exaggerated facial expressions, and seemed less than pleased when the defense called a parade of witnesses to the stand to testify to Mickey's troubled youth and family life.

The jury did not take much time reaching a verdict and the judge set sentencing for three weeks. As that date approached, Jeanne was apprehensive. Although she knew she would be given the chance to ask for a harsh penalty—the DA had assured her that he would press for the maximum—still she hated the idea that she would again face Mickey in court. During the trial, she was bothered by his stares and the exaggerated facial expressions and gestures of disbelief when she testified. She had difficulty getting his image out of her mind and frequently woke up during the night in a cold sweat. The sentencing date finally arrived, and the DA kept his promise. He made a vivid and strong pitch for the maximum. Sentencing Mickey to 10 to 20 years, the judge noted that the crime was terrible and that he hoped Mickey would serve the full duration of his sentence.

EPILOGUE

As Jeanne tried to regain her emotional health, she commented that the sentences, although severe, would never be severe enough to compensate for the hurt she and her family had suffered. Her daughters and husband had all been affected by the crime and were struggling to return to the life they enjoyed before the shock of the attack. As she reviewed the trial with a friend, Jeanne observed that the trial experience was terrible. Although she recognized that the defense attorneys were quite deferential and even sometimes embarrassed by their client (Mickey had asked for and received a different attorney halfway during the trial), she observed that Mickey's face and posture at trial would stay with her forever. She wondered, perhaps, if it would have been better if he, too, had plead guilty. But then, five to nine didn't sound very long.

DISCUSSION QUESTIONS

1. What did the defendant, Sam, gain by pleading guilty? Was there any negotiation or exchange in that plea?
2. Are all guilty pleas negotiated? Can you think of any circumstances that might prompt a defendant to plead guilty without any negotiations?
3. What did Mickey gain by going to trial? Was the court justified in sentencing Mickey more severely than Sam? What might account for the disparity in sentences?
4. What effect did Mickey's trial have on the victim, Jeanne?
5. Was plea bargaining appropriate in this crime? Should the state have pursued trials for both defendants?
6. What does the victim gain or lose by the criminal trial?

SUGGESTED READING
"PLEA BARGAINING AIN'T SO BAD"

Blumberg, Abraham 5.
   1967 "The Practice of Law as a Confidence Game: Organizational Co-optation of a Profession." *Law and Society Review* I: 15-39.
   The now classic analysis of the plea bargaining process, especially as it contravenes the tenets of the adversarial system. Blumberg directs considerable attention to the legal profession and its support of a system of bargain justice.

Heumann, Milton
   1978 *Plea Bargaining: The Experiences of Prosecutors, Judges, and Defense Attorneys.* Chicago: University of Chicago Press.
   An extensive study of plea bargaining in Connecticut that calls some of the standing assessments into question and focuses on the degree to which new attorneys adapt to court processes and norms.

Note
   1970 "The Unconstitutionality of Plea Bargaining." *Harvard Law Review* 83: 1387.
   The frequently cited law review article that attacked the constitutional status of plea bargaining. The thesis generated considerable interest in and appeared to have influenced the 1973 recommendation of the National Advisory Commission on Criminal Justice Standards and Goals that called for the elimination of plea bargaining.

Rhodes, William M.
   1978 *Plea Bargaining: Who Gains? Who Loses?* Washington, D.C.: Institute for Law and Social Research.
   An extensive statistical analysis of the effects of plea bargaining. Rhodes argues that plea bargaining practices meet both due process and crime control objectives, and that trials are very expensive in comparison to guilty plea settlements.

Case Ten

I'm Really Torn

THE ISSUE

Augustus, or "Gus" Campbell was obviously upset. Earlier he had called the office of the State Bar Association and asked for some assistance with a particular question of legal ethics. Specifically, Gus wanted to know if he could tell the appropriate authorities about a client's "confession," or did the bar's code of professional conduct prohibit such a breach of lawyer-client confidentiality. Although Gus did not reveal the identity of his client, and the case conceivably could have fit many others in the state criminal justice system, he was referring to one Tyler Jackson.

Tyler Jackson was a young con with a rap sheet as long as any of the more serious inmates in the state's maximum security prison. With a string of felonies, probation and parole violations, and violent behavior to his dubious credit, he was currently incarcerated for felony murder. Although Tyler had not been convicted of the actual killing, he was imprisoned as an accomplice. The sentencing judge did not take kindly to Tyler's criminal history and sentenced him to life imprisonment, a fairly substantial term for the driver of a getaway car.

Gus was privy to Tyler's information because he was serving as his attorney on appeal. Actually, lengthy appeals of convictions such as Tyler's were not very common, but Tyler's case involved an issue of jury selection that higher courts were interested in exploring. So, the state's Indigent Defense Council had assigned him the appeal. As a full-time staff member of the defense council, Gus had extensive appellate experience.

THE CRIME

Some three years prior to his most recent conversation with Gus Campbell, Tyler Jackson was picked up for murder. He and his friend, Curtis Barrow, were identified from a police "mug book" as the pair who robbed a convenience store and killed a clerk early one Saturday evening. From all accounts, the crime was rather typical albeit still terrible. A tall, thin, white man entered the store, put a gun to the clerk's head, and demanded the contents of the register. Although the robber did not pull the trigger, he did hit the clerk over the head, inflicting sufficient injury to cause death a few days later. As the robber left the store, a customer drove up, catching a glimpse of the robber, car, and driver.

When interviewed by police, the customer identified Curtis Barrow as the robber and Tyler Jackson as the driver of the car. Police lost no time in tracking the pair down because they had not only substantial criminal records, but also fairly predictable habits and living arrangements. Tyler Jackson was picked up first and admitted to driving the car. Additionally, he pointed to Curtis Barrow as the robber.

Tyler Jackson and Curtis Barrow were both tried for felony murder and armed robbery. A public defender, Susan Waycross, initially handled both of their cases, but they were split when it became apparent that at least one of the two would testify against the other. Surprisingly, both cases went to trial. Jackson and Barrow changed their stories so often that Waycross and Wayne Linden, Barrow's attorney, could not get either one to agree on any detail of the case, much less the terms of a plea negotiation.

Tyler Jackson was tried first and took the stand in his own defense. His final story was somewhat different from earlier versions, but he stuck to it through the trial. Specifically, he charged that he and Barrow had stopped to pick up some cigarettes and that Barrow, unknown to him, proceeded to pull off an armed robbery. Jackson insisted that he did not see the gun in Barrow's jacket pocket, nor did he have any idea that his friend was thinking about the crime. Insisting that Barrow ran out and told him to move fast or they both would be in trouble, Jackson repeated that he was an accomplice but an innocent one. Furthermore, he emphasized that he knew nothing of the clerk's head injury.

At his trial, Barrow offered a different story. He insisted that he had not even been with Jackson that evening and had nothing to do with any robbery. His case, however, was complicated by the fact that Jackson testified against him and by the customer who served as a witness in each trial and who identified him as the robber. Both Barrow and Jackson were convicted of the same crimes in separate trials, although the judge sentenced Jackson to a less severe term than Barrow. Specifically, Jackson received a life term while Barrow got death.

THE APPEAL

Barrow's attorney was appealing his conviction, standard in death penalty litigation, but Wayne Linden was worried because there didn't seem to be a strong procedural question and substantively, Barrow only complained that "he was framed," a common allegation. In contrast, Jackson seemed to have a stronger basis for appeal. There were questions about the prosecutor's handling of jury selection and several attorneys in the Indigent Defense Council's office thought that this offered potentially strong grounds for appeal.

In the course of several conversations with his appellate lawyer, Gus Campbell, Jackson offered a startling revelation. "Barrow had nothing to do with that store robbery. Me and my kid brother actually pulled it off. My kid brother looks a lot like Barrow, so when the cops came looking for me, I thought he would make an easy fall guy. I mean, my kid brother has never been in trouble before. He's just down and out of luck and needed a little cash to tide himself over. He panicked and hit that clerk. He was no risk to get into more trouble and I just couldn't bear the picture of him going to prison. It'd break my mother's heart." With some additional probing on Campbell's part, he put some of the pieces of the story together. Jackson did drive the getaway car but his younger brother, Travis, had actually entered the store, put the gun to the clerk's head, and demanded the money. Barrow was easy to pin the blame on because he not only resembled Tyler's brother in an uncanny way, but he also had no excuse or alibi for the evening in question, and Tyler knew it. Specifically, Barrow had been drinking heavily earlier in the afternoon and Tyler left him in his apartment—dead drunk and sleeping one hour before the robbery. Since no one saw, or would later admit to seeing, Tyler bring Curtis home, Barrow was without a convincing case to put to the jury. More important, he couldn't remember anything of the day of the crime.

GUS'S DILEMMA

Gus was obviously upset with Tyler's story. "Don't tell anyone about this," he cautioned, "until I have time to think things over. And don't mention this to any of your prison cronies, either." Leaving the prison after his meeting, Gus went home and started what would become several days of anguish and deliberation. During this time, he called the bar association's office to put a "hypothetical" to the staff. Gus's hypothetical involved a lawyer who was handling a case on appeal. Not privy to earlier conversations and contact at the trial level, Gus's hypothetical lawyer had learned that his client had fingered an innocent man. Could he, as the appellate attorney, reveal this conversation to the appropriate authorities and try to secure an innocent man's release from prison or was he bound by legal ethics to keep his mouth shut?

The bar association's advice did not offer much comfort. If Gus's hypothetical lawyer were working with this client prior to trial, then he could not let him take the stand and offer perjurious testimony. If his client insisted, then the lawyer would be bound to resign from the case and/or notify the judge. However, on appeal with no previous knowledge of the perjured testimony, the lawyer was bound to keep his mouth shut and work to his client's advantage, namely to try to secure an acquittal or a new trial on the procedural issue raised in jury selection. "Defend the principle of fair procedure in the appeal," the staff member advised, "and try to forget about the alleged confession. It's the other guy's attorney's job to try and secure an appeal for his client."

Gus was not relieved by this conversation because he knew that Barrow didn't have much of a chance on appeal. Furthermore, he knew that if Jackson were telling the truth now, not only was an innocent man spending a lot of time in prison but a guilty one was free to roam the streets. "I'm really torn," he said to no one in particular when he hung up the phone.

THE EPILOGUE

Tyler Jackson didn't have very many visitors in prison—even his brother failed to put in an occasional appearance. However, the prison chaplain had taken notice of the inmate and in the course of time had spent several hours with him in conversation and, in some respects, counseling. Tyler offered the same confession to the chaplain, an elderly Methodist minister, who at first, thought it was just a tale to pass the time. With repeated telling, however, the minister became convinced that Tyler was telling the truth. Adopting a pastoral stance, he urged Tyler to make the confession official and "do the right thing."

In relatively short order, Tyler's confession began to make the rounds of the prison and eventually to the more secluded death row wing. Curtis Barrow shared the rumor with his attorney who then asked prison authorities if he could speak with Jackson. The staff agreed and Wayne Linden met with Jackson. After Jackson repeated the story, Linden asked him if he would testify to that effect in a sworn deposition or affidavit. Tyler agreed, although he was disturbed by the fact that his kid brother would eventually join him in prison. This disappointment, however, was muted by Travis' failure to even visit Tyler in the three years that had passed since the crime.

Gus Campbell was upset when he learned that Linden had visited his client and was even more distraught when he heard that Tyler had agreed to help him with Barrow's appeal. There was, however, little he could do to limit the damage as Tyler's confession amounted to new evidence and Linden would later have little trouble winning a new trial.

At the new trial, Barrow once again testified in his own defense. Jackson, with the chaplain's encouragement, took the stand and repeated his now commonly heard confession. The jury acquitted Barrow, while Tyler's brother Travis, would later be convicted of felony murder. He soon joined his brother in prison, however, as he was not eligible for the death penalty. When the clerk had been murdered, Travis was only fifteen.

DISCUSSION QUESTIONS

1. What should Gus Campbell have done when confronted with the information of his client's (Tyler Jackson) knowledge that Curtis Barrow was innocent of the crime he had been sent to death for?
2. Does lawyer-client confidentiality normally preclude any effort on Gus's part to share information on Barrow's innocence with the appropriate authorities?
3. What should Gus Campbell do as Tyler Jackson's lawyer? Specifically, what objectives should he try to realize? Are these identical to those he tried to realize?
4. What is required for a criminal defense? Should Gus Campbell have cautioned Tyler, "Don' t tell this to anyone?" Should Curtis Barrow's lawyer, Wayne Linden, have asked to speak with Tyler Jackson without informing Gus Campbell? What responsibilities did Linden have for his client in this regard?

SUGGESTED READING
"I'M REALLY TORN"

Hazard, Geoffrey C., Jr.
1978   *Ethics in the Practice of Law*. New Haven, Connecticut: Yale University Press.

A collection of essays on the topic of legal ethics by one of the most prominent authorities in the field. Hazard discusses the adversarial system, conflict of interest issues, institutional and personal clients, and the lawyer's moral obligations to his/her client.

Partridge, Anthony and Gordon Bermant
1978   *The Quality of Advocacy in the Federal Courts*. Washington, D.C.: Federal Judicial Center.

A comprehensive assessment of the quality of legal representation in the nation's federal courts, this report was issued to the Committee of the Judicial Conference of the United States to Consider Standards for Admission to Practice in the Federal Courts.

Robinson, Paul H.
1988   *Fundamentals of Criminal Law*. Boston: Little, Brown.

A comprehensive introduction to substantive criminal law. The two sections in Chapter 5 provide a useful review of the law of homicide with specific attention to felony murder in Section 19.

van den Haag, Ernest and John P. Conrad
1983   *The Death Penalty: A Debate*. New York: Plenum Press.

Van den Haag offers a defense of capital punishment, while Conrad argues the opposite position. The debate offers an interesting summary of the issues underlying capital punishment and fairly concise reviews of the two conflicting opinions.

Wishman, Seymour
1981   *Confessions of a Criminal Lawyer*. New York: Penguin Books.

A journalistic-like description of one criminal lawyer's experiences. Readers need to be reminded that this represents only one view of the profession and that the autobiographical style limits the generalizability of the author's conclusions.

PART THREE

Corrections

Introduction

Corrections constitutes the third major component of the criminal justice system and encompasses a variety of organizations. In state systems, these include jails that are run by local governments (typically cities and counties), prisons that are administered by state agencies, and a range of alternatives that are controlled by local and state offices. The latter is dominated by probation and parole, although a variety of other alternatives to incarceration (e.g., halfway houses, work-release programs, drug rehabilitation centers, shock probation) have captured both public and professional attention in recent years. On the federal level, corrections include the U.S. prison system and probation. Since the U.S. Parole Board was phased out of existence with the passage of federal sentencing guidelines, that institution has assumed far less importance in the federal system.

Technically, the correctional process begins with sentencing when the presiding judge imposes the penalty for the convicted offense. Although judicial sentencing has received considerable attention for some time, the penalties imposed are not necessarily the ones implemented. Early releases for good behavior while incarcerated, parole releases, and other policy programs impact the sentences judges impose. An additional effect is the manner in which correctional agencies operate and the resources that shape their ability to carry out the court's sentence.

Contemporary corrections is, in many ways, operating at crisis capacity. Jails and prisons are overcrowded, agency administrators lobby consistently for more resources, and alternatives to costly incarceration are defined and applied. Complicating these efforts is the fact that there seems to be considerable public support for punitive prison terms and little appreciation of both the limits of criminal law and the correctional system.

To a very real degree, all of these issues are reflected in the five cases in this section. The first, *Too Much Discretion,* focuses on the probation process with special attention to the revocation of this alternative to incarceration. As the case details, probation officers have considerable discretion in revocation as probationer recall depends on some initial recommendation by the case officer. *Too Much Discretion* speaks to this discretion and to the power vested in the sentencing judge who makes the final determination on probation revocation. As such, the case deals with issues central to the general criminal justice system and the correctional process. These include the nature of discretionary authority, sentence disparities, the process of revocation, and the relationships or work groups within a criminal court.

Prison overcrowding dominates the next two cases, *Interview With Commissioner Allen* and *Looking for State Prison*. In the interview, a newspaper reporter is speaking with a state corrections commissioner in an effort to learn more about the population crisis in the state prisons. As Commissioner Allen explains, prison overcrowding is affected by a variety of things and not amenable to simple solutions. In addition to the obvious dependance on the legislature, the corrections department must try to deal with competing public policies for criminal law and with an institutional structure that has long been neglected in state politics.

A similar theme is highlighted in *Looking for State Prison,* although the focus is quite different. In this case, attention is directed to a convicted felon who is sentenced to an experimental 90-day shock probation program. Since that alternative program is crowded, the convict must wait in a local jail. When 90 days pass, the convict takes the law into his own hands, so to speak, and literally walks out of the jail toward the state facility where he was supposed to serve his actual sentence. The case illustrates several dimensions of the correctional process and the overcrowding problem. Included are the effects on individual prisoners and the interrelated character of the criminal justice system. Additionally the case directs the reader's attention to a specific alternative to incarceration and the difficulties associated with its implementation.

Since the majority of states still maintain some type of early release or parole system, it is necessary to consider that institution in any text designed to cover major topics in criminal justice. *I'll See You Monday* details the story of one parolee and the decisions his parole officer made with regard to his case. Similar to probation, parole involves a conditional form of release with substantial discretionary authority vested in supervising officers. In contrast, however, parole is not administered by courts but typically by administrative agencies operating within or in close proximity to state correctional agencies. Both probation and parole processes, however, are directed by some due process standards, although these rights are not as extensively defined in the correctional arena as suspect rights are in the courts. *I'll See You Monday* raises some related due process concerns, as well as the discretionary power vested in parole authorities and the problems associated with the supervision of conditionally released felons.

An important issue related to the general standard of due process in criminal justice is the confidentiality of defendant and prisoner records. For many years, many state agencies either operated their own research divisions (e.g., California) or allowed researchers considerable access to official records and files. With the advent of federal privacy standards, however, many police, court, and correctional agencies adopted guidelines for the release of confidential records. Although access still depends to some degree on the discretionary authority of agency heads, some have regularized the process in an effort to see that uniform standards are applied. *I Just Need the Data* tells the story of one researcher who was interested in gaining access to a state prison's inmate records and in interviewing a subgroup of the prison population. As the case documents, the researcher's subject was controversial and the agency uncomfortable with her request. However the reader judges the merits of her application—and the case calls for such determinations—the story illustrates the efforts correctional agencies have taken to project inmate privacy and the degree to which uniform procedures have helped or hindered that effort and the general research agenda.

The following chart outlines the five cases included in this section and draws the reader's attention to the major concepts and issues reflected in each. Again, it is the authors' expectation that students will not only offer their own assessments or judgments of the decisions at hand, but also search for other material or cases to use as points of comparison.

PART THREE: CORRECTIONS

Case Title	Central Subject	Concepts/Issues
Too Much Discretion	probation revocation	probation officer discretion judicial revocation discretion technical probation violation sentencing disparities court relationships
Interview With Commissioner Allen	prison overcrowding	causes/solutions: prison overcrowding interrelated dimensions of criminal justice
Looking for State Prison	prison and jail overcrowding	structure/function in correctional systems alternatives to incarceration
I'll See You Monday	parole and parole revocation	parole revocation parole supervision parole officer discretion conditional release due process
I Just Need the Data	privacy and criminal justice	privacy of inmate records research access to public agency data professionalism

Case Eleven

Too Much Discretion

PART ONE

Rich Delgato slumped on a bench in the first floor hallway of the sweltering Martin County Courthouse. By mid-morning, the building's feeble air conditioning system had already yielded to the oppressive August heat. "Baling wire and twine," Delgato thought to himself as he sipped his soda and speculated about the composition of materials that held the air conditioning system together. He had decided to take a moment to gather his thoughts after a frustrating session before Judge MacMichael. MacMichael's inability to adhere to a consistent policy in the treatment of probation violators was bewildering.

The judge had just adjourned a resentencing hearing for one of Delgato's probationers, a habitual traffic violator, who had received a mere two-year extension on his probation. This man, accompanied by a lawyer who aggressively attacked both the local sheriff's department and especially the probation office, pleaded his case by appealing to the judge's "humanity and common decency." The strategy had obviously worked.

Only two weeks earlier, another probationer had gone before Judge MacMichael on *exactly* the same charge. The judge had sentenced this man to a four-year prison sentence to be followed by an additional six years on probation. A month earlier, this man had been arrested by the Verde City police for driving with a suspended driver's license. Since he was also serving a term on probation as a habitual traffic violator, his arrest led to a warrant being issued for a violation of the conditions of his probation. People arrested under probation warrants were not ordinarily permitted to post bond, so Delgato's client had been held in the county jail since the time of his arrest. Garbed in the standard prison jump suit, the man was transported directly from the courthouse to one of the state's medium security institutions to begin serving his time. Considered together, an inequity seemed to exist in the way the two cases were handled.

The source of Rich Delgato's frustration with Judge MacMichael was the judge's apparent indifference to the biases built into the state's procedures for dealing with people charged with violations of the conditions of probation. The first man resentenced by MacMichael was José Rivera, who was poor, Hispanic, and who had obvious difficulty understanding the operation of the legal system. Delgato felt that the system had a marked tendency to deal more severely with people like Rivera than it did with individuals who were better prepared to defend themselves against charges stemming from probation violations.

Although Judge MacMichael apparently did not harbor any clear-cut prejudices against the poor or minorities, he was extremely intolerant of "jailhouse lawyering" by defendants who appeared before him. The judge failed to appreciate that indigent persons appearing on probation warrants were often compelled to defend themselves against charges stemming from alleged probation violations. Under state policy (and presumably constitutional law), indigent probationers had no inherent right to appointed counsel. In Martin County, poor people inevitably appeared without counsel unless someone was willing to hire an attorney for them. Delgato had seen many occasions where indigent probationers would receive prison time simply because they could not—on their own ability—provide a plausible argument for a return to probationary status.

Judge Theodore MacMichael thought that the public had a right to expect him to fully exercise his judicial experience when deciding the outcome of cases that came before him. It had been twenty-five years since he had been appointed to a judgeship in the Grandview Circuit (which included Martin County), and now the judge felt that his obligations to the community were as great or greater than they had ever been.

Three problems were particularly irksome to Judge MacMichael, each of which posed substantial threats to his ability to competently administer justice in the Grandview Circuit. First, there was the problem of outsiders to the community, particularly defense lawyers from other cities, who would challenge the judge's prerogative to base decisions on longstanding and well-understood criteria of what was best for the local community. Rarely did the judge find the arrogance of "outsiders" to be an asset to criminal defendants.

Second, the judge was fully aware that the criminal justice system—police and sheriff's departments, district attorney's offices, probation and parole offices—was a consituency all its own. The only real stability in the system was in the sheriff's offices and even here this was usually limited to the tenure of the sheriff himself. Aside from the sheriffs, then, the judge was compelled to deal with innumerable problems brought before him by politically motivated attorneys, law enforcement "hotshots," and a whole variety of community-based correctional people who seemed to understand state correctional policies a whole lot better than they understood the operation of the judicial system.

Lastly, there was the perpetually present assortment of riffraff, street hustlers, drunks, and other unsavory types who used their court appearances as an opportunity to engage in the practice of law. MacMichael was less offended by the inane and inarticulate defenses offered in the face of obvious guilt, than he was by the incredible waste of time and court resources that had to be expended on such matters. For such cases, the judge invoked a simple maxim: "They take up my time, I'll take up some of theirs!"

In Judge MacMichael's mind, the administration of justice was straightforward, if it was not in fact a matter of the simple determination of guilt or innocence. All of the criminal law and procedure in the world could not save a court system from the inability or unwillingness of an experienced judge to use such experience to guide appropriate judgments. For MacMichael, the biggest problems in the court system were those influences that hindered or prevented a judge from getting on with his work. The clearer he could make his feelings known in this regard, the more efficient and just the system was likely to be.

Probation work in the Grandview Circuit was beset by the same problems that faced community-based corrections in many other areas of the country. Case loads were unmanageably large, officers often felt unappreciated and underpaid, and the typical probationer was either a person who was destined to have no more than a single brush with the law or one consumed by a consistent pattern of chronic criminality. This latter group was the bane of probation work. These people were usually not violent offenders, but individuals who, for a variety of reasons, seemed incapable of staying out of trouble with the law. Recently their numbers had swollen because of major changes in the state's response to drunk driving. Stricter enforcement combined with more severe sentences had led to the discovery of a new class of "criminals:" the chronic drinking driver. Rich Delgato had a large number of these people on his case load. Ordinarily, they had three or more convictions for driving under the influence and some combination of associated charges, such as driving with a suspended operator's license, no liability insurance, and similar charges. The "master charge" reflective of the syndrome was a conviction as a "habitual violator," a charge that always drew some jail time followed by a lengthy period on probation.

The cases that formed the core of Delgato's displeasure with Judge MacMichael were of this sort. In the most recent case, a metalworker by the name of Mike Seiler was on probation for several drinking and driving-related incidents that eventually led to a habitual violator conviction, a jail sentence, $1,000 fine, and six years probation. On the evening that he was arrested, Seiler was returning from his job at a plant that manufactured heating and air conditioning duct work. He lived in a town about 20 miles from the plant; this presented a problem. Seiler had received a one-year suspension of his driver's license and had been warned by Delgato that a rearrest on traffic charges could lead to a revocation of his probation. Seiler had been lucky for he was able to strike a deal with a neighbor and coworker who would drive Seiler's car on the trip to and from work.

On the evening that he was arrested, Seiler was driving home from work because his coworker had succumbed to stomach flu and both men felt that having Seiler take the wheel was worth the risk. Unfortunately, Seiler made the mistake of rolling through a stop sign (i.e., failure to come to a complete stop) in full view of a sheriff's deputy. Given that Seiler was driving with a suspended license, the deputy had no choice but to arrest Seiler and take him to the Martin County Jail. Two days later, Seiler was served with a warrant for violation of the terms of his probation and thus was constrained to remain in the county jail.

Fortunately for Seiler, both the county sheriff and a very competent attorney came to his aid. In a highly unorthodox move, Judge MacMichael agreed to the attorney's request to have the sheriff, Rich Delgato, Mike Seiler, and the attorney meet for an informal "conference" in the judge's office to discuss a pretrial release from jail. In Delgato's mind, state law was very clear in stating that persons arrested on probation warrants were to be confined without bond until there was a resentencing hearing on their case. Nevertheless, MacMichael listened attentively as the sheriff and attorney argued that it was imperative that Seiler be allowed to return to work especially in light of the harmless and trivial nature of the incident that led to his recent traffic arrest.

When MacMichael agreed to release Seiler, Rich Delgato knew that little would come of the more serious charge that an habitual violator had violated the conditions of his probation. This was indeed the case as Judge MacMichael gently cautioned Seiler about the potentially serious nature of traffic offenses in his particular case. After this, MacMichael added two meaningless years to Seiler's term on probation.

José Rivera was not so lucky. Rivera's history of trouble with the law was very similar to Seiler's. He had several DUI convictions on his record and some traffic violations. These had led to conviction on an habitual violator charge. He too was employed and under probation supervision. Rivera worked full time as a yardman at a local lumberyard and, like Seiler, was dependent on his coworkers for his means of transportation to work and from one work site to another. He was arrested during working hours when he was stopped while driving a flatbed delivery truck owned by the lumber company. For reasons that were not clear to anyone, four of Rivera's coworkers, all of whom had valid driver's licenses, were riding on the bed of the truck when Rivera was arrested.

After his arrest, the events surrounding Rivera's case unfolded in a fashion similar to Seiler's. He too had been arrested initially on a charge of driving with a suspended license. This was followed by a warrant for his arrest on allegations of violating the conditions of his probation, specifically, being rearrested after an habitual violator conviction. Unlike Seiler, however, Rivera had not been able to afford an attorney and thus was forced to appear before Judge MacMichael without legal representation. Judge MacMichael was not impressed by Rivera's inarticulate pleadings and was even less impressed by his inability to provide an account of why he, in the presence of four coworkers, was driving with a suspended driver's license. Rich Delgato as the supervising probation officer was able to give an objective account of his clients excellent, recent work history, but as initiator of the arrest warrant, Delgato was in a poor position to recommend that Rivera not be sanctioned for his infraction of the rules of probation. As a consequence, MacMichael sentenced Rivera to a four-year prison term (with two to serve) and extended his post-incarceration probation to six years. At the time, Delgato did not have a great deal of sympathy for Rivera since he would not actually serve more than about six months in jail, and he should have known better than to have stupidly jumped behind the wheel of a truck for no apparent good reason. Still, the notion that Rivera might have fared better had he had an attorney present at his resentencing hearing nagged at Delgato. It would be weeks later before it really dawned on him that Rivera represented a whole class of people who might be disadvantaged in Judge MacMichael's court.

PART TWO

"You're just too quick with the ol' warrants," Mike Seiler exclaimed, as he passed Rich Delgato in the courthouse hallway. "Man, if you don't cut dudes some slack, the judge will." Delgato pitched the empty soda can in the trash as he left the courthouse not far behind Seiler and his attorney. Seiler's comments had come across less as a taunt and more as a much experienced probationer's attempt to tell his supervisor how to do his job.

Delgato's operating ethos had never been directly challenged either by his own supervisors or any of the judges who presided over the Grandview Circuit. Although he realized his position granted him much discretionary authority, Delgato tried as much as possible to keep his own exercise of discretion in check. In general, Delgato saw two major threats to the unbridled use of discretion by a probation officer. On the one hand, there was the whole business of the probationer taking the instructions of the probation officer and the rules of probation supervision seriously. Delgato figured that supervision would be more difficult in the long run if probationers were ever led to believe that the form and content of probation supervision were negotiable. Delgato had known other officers who had lost almost all control over their clients simply because they had been too willing to relax the rules of supervision in too many separate and discrete situations. On the other hand, there was the issue of fair and equitable treatment. Delgato questioned the appropriateness of discretionary supervision because from one case to the next, there was the constant potential for some supervisors to receive more slack than others. This was part of Delgato's beef with Judge MacMichael. The judge was *so* prone to think only of the immediate case, that he lost all sense of perspective on what people ought to be able to expect from his decisions generally.

Dealing with habitual violators was a good example of how Delgato managed his discretion. All probationers, no matter what the nature of their problem with the law, were expected to stay out of trouble. Needless to say, this was especially so with habitual violators. Delgato's policy was to issue warrants for all violations of probation by habitual violators who had been rearrested. To enforce this policy required fairly rigorous enforcement on Delgato's part. Law enforcement agencies within the county could not be relied upon to notify the probation office when a probationer had been arrested. Non-DUI traffic offenses simply did not concern police departments sufficiently to spur a detailed investigation of an arrestee's background. If Delgato was to learn of these arrests, it was his duty to contact the police departments to see if any of his clients had had contacts with any of the various departments. In practicality, this meant that Delgato needed to visit each station in the county at least once or twice a week and examine the arrest books to see if the names of any of his clients appeared.

If Delgato noted the name of one of his clients, he had a number of choices. He could ignore the incident (which was antithetical to the whole purpose of examining the books in the first place). He could contact the individual and warn them informally that they might be placing their probationary status in jeopardy. He could also formally reprimand the probationer and place a written report of the reprimand in the probationer's file. Last, he could have a warrant served for the individual's arrest and have them held until a resentencing hearing could be conducted to give full consideration to the charges.

Although the last course of action superficially appeared to be the most severe, it was also the most fair—or at least Delgato had thought so up until the recent incidents with Rivera and Seiler. Now Delgato was not so sure of himself. As Delgato pulled out of the courthouse parking lot, Seiler's comments reverberated in his head. The upshot of Seiler's remarks was clear: if Delgato didn't exercise discretion in doing his job, MacMichael would adjust to this by exercising more discretion in his role. Delgato wondered whether it was possible that he was in some way at fault for the behavior he criticized in MacMichael. This was not a happy thought.

DISCUSSION QUESTIONS

1. Should the probation officer, Rich Delgato, have initiated revocation proceedings against José Rivera and Mike Seiler?
2. What was the source of Rich Delgato's frustration with Judge MacMichael?
3. Were Delgato's concerns about Judge MacMichael's revocation penalties warranted?
4. What might have contributed to the judge's decisions in the cases of José Rivera and Mike Seiler?
5. Does Rich Delgato, the probation officer, have too much discretion? Does the judge?
6. How can the discretionary authority of the probation office and the judge be directed?

SUGGESTED READING
"TOO MUCH DISCRETION"

Clear, Todd
  1979 "Three Dilemmas in Community Supervision." *Prison Journal.* 59: 3-16.

  Problems can arise in probation supervision over three sometimes conflicting aspects of probation: 1) its essential purpose; 2) the methods used to select offenders for probation supervision; and 3) appropriate methods of supervision. Clear emphasizes the unique nature of discretion in probation work and the pervasive influence it has at all decision points within the process.

Czajkoski, Eugene H.
  1973 "Exposing the Quasi-Judicial Role of the Probation Officer." *Federal Probation.* 37: 9-13.

  The probation officer has tremendous potential influence on the treatment of criminal offenders beginning with the presentence investigation through all phases of community-based correction. The author analyzes the decision-making function of probation work through each stage of the probation process. The discussion of the role of the probation officer in revocation proceedings is especially important.

Katz, Janet

  1982 "The Attitudes and Decisions of Probation Officers." *Criminal Justice and Behavior.* 9: 455-475.

  This article examines how probation officers' attitudes toward their work influences the recommendations that they make for case dispositions. Katz finds that in addition to legally relevant criteria, attitudes have a significant impact on probation officer decision-making.

Klockars, Carl

  1972 "A Theory of Probation Supervision." *Journal of Criminal Law, Criminology, and Police Science.* 63: 550-557.

  Klockars provides a typology of four working philosophies that underlie probation supervision. These differing philosophies set up the "treatment-control dilemma" that poses major obstacles to effective supervision. Klockars outlines a strategy of effective supervision in response to this dilemma based on a model of social exchange.

Rosecrance, John

  1985 "The Probation Officer's Search for Credibility: Ball Park Recommendations." *Crime and Delinquency.* 31: 539-554

  Although focused primarily on the presentence investigation process, this article vividly depicts the problems probation officers face having their recommendations taken seriously. The working relationship between the sentencing judge and the probation officer is a path of interaction that receives special scrutiny in this article.

Rountree, George A., Dan W. Edwards and Jack B. Parker.

  1984 "A Study of the Personal Characteristics of Probationers as Related to Recidivism." *Journal of Offender Counseling Services and Rehabilitation.* 8: 53-61.

  This is a study of factors related to individuals success or failure on probation. The authors found that 14% of their sample had had their probation revoked. Factors such as prior record, age at first arrest, number of prior arrests, and offender classification were among those variables associated with recidivism.

Case Twelve

Interview With Commissioner Allen

My name is Helen Bennett. I am a staff reporter for the *Capitol City News,* an east coast daily. My major area of reporting responsibility is state government, and today I have an early morning appointment with a prominent state official.

Daniel G. Allen has been the Commissioner of the State Department of Corrections for 15 years. Prior to becoming the chief administrator of this large state agency, Commissioner Allen was an associate director of the state board of industrial development and, before that, the planning and budget director of the state corrections agency. He has survived three governors. He avoids the media; maybe that's why he's lasted so long.

I am a little reluctant about this morning's interview. It's hard to make interesting reading out of the state prison system. Our readership is barely interested in national and local politics! So, the state government area generally leaves them cold. But prisons! The public likes to forget about criminals once they're caught and locked up. Frankly, so do I.

I wouldn't have set up the interview if it wasn't for the big budget increase that Commissioner Allen is seeking. The legislature was in a hoopla last week when he told them he wants $100 million in new prison construction. That little bombshell got everybody's attention. I decided that I'd better find out what all of this budget busting is all about.

I'll give the man one thing: he sure works hard. Reporters aren't used to 7:30 a.m. meetings. But he was so heavily scheduled that this was the only time that we could find on his calendar. In any case, the early start helped me miss the morning rush hour traffic. I even found a parking place near the state capitol.

Well, it's 7:15 and I've just been handed the bureaucracy's mandatory styro-foam cup of coffee. I shouldn't complain, some agencies are so cold to the press that we don't even get coffee. Oops! This must be him now. Funny, I thought he'd be taller.

This case was written by Professor George Cox of Georgia Southern College

BENNETT   Good morning, Commissioner.

ALLEN   Good morning. You must be Helen Bennett.

BENNETT   Guilty as charged.

ALLEN   No, I like your stuff. You usually give us a fair shake. I read your series on women in prison last year. It was pretty well balanced, for a reporter.

BENNETT   Thanks, I think. Was the women's piece too critical?

ALLEN   Criticism is something we get lots of. Critics and inmates, we're loaded with both. Anyway, let's not stand out here in the hall. I can at least offer you a seat.

We went in and sat down in his large but not luxurious office. He hung up his coat and then surprised me by not heading behind his desk. I would have guessed that he would have put it between us.

Instead, we sat in two reasonably comfortable armchairs next to a little coffee table near the window. It was raining outside, that steady drizzle that makes running around town a reporter's nightmare. He rolled up his shirtsleeves, and we waded into the state prison crisis.

BENNETT   Well, Commissioner, let's start with the question of the hour. Why do the people of this state need to spend $100 million on new prisons?

ALLEN   That's how much five new institutions cost.

BENNETT   Twenty million dollars sounds like a lot for a prison. And $100 million could buy a lot of education or highways or human services that our law-abiding citizens need.

ALLEN   Prisons are expensive, and they're getting more costly to build every year. As for your other point, I want good schools and highways and services as much as you do, but we're in a real crisis in the state prison system.

BENNETT   "Crisis." We hear that word a lot from government officials. What are we really talking about here, fewer color TVs or tennis courts for criminals?

ALLEN   Far from it! State prisons are having trouble simply feeding, housing, and supervising all the people the courts are sending us.

BENNETT   Oh? Are you blaming the courts for your budget needs?

ALLEN   I'm not "blaming" anyone, Ms. Bennett! It's my responsibility to see to it that offenders are properly supervised and cared for after they're convicted. I can't do my job when we have twice as many people in our prisons as they were designed to hold.

The Commissioner got up from his seat and walked over to his desk. He began looking through a stack of papers on the far left corner away from where we'd been sitting. He looked a little red in the face. Maybe I was pushing too hard for so early in the interview and for so early in the morning. He found what he was looking for and came back over to the sitting area.

BENNETT   I didn't mean to suggest that you were trying to find a scapegoat in the judiciary.

ALLEN   Well, thanks for that at least. These are the current and projected figures for our inmate population. As you can see from the line graph, the numbers just keep going up and up. And we can hold only so many people in our current buildings.

BENNETT   The crime rate in this state must really be getting bad.

ALLEN   Not really. My reading of the standard kinds of crime reports is that the overall crime rate is holding fairly steady. Figures for particular kinds of crime are up and down, of course. But basically, we're no worse off in terms of the crime rate than we were ten years ago.

BENNETT   Then the problem is harsher sentencing.

ALLEN   Well, harsher is a value judgment, and it's not my place to judge the judges. The criminal code has been changed in some important ways in recent years. The judges actually have less discretion today than they had say a decade ago.

BENNETT   This is getting a little complicated.

ALLEN   Sure it's complicated. Let me give you a basic word picture of how the prison population is determined. Think of a swimming pool. When it's empty, that's our institutional capacity. We can hold only so many people. Now imagine that we turn on the water inflow to the pool. That's the inmates coming from the courts. They literally come in a steady flow. Week in and week out, new prisoners come to us from the courts. Many of them from temporary confinement in local jails.

BENNETT   You don't run the jails, right?

ALLEN   Right. Those facilities are operated by local governments. The person over the jail might be the county sheriff or a local jail administrator.

BENNETT   They have their own institutional problems, right?

ALLEN   Yes and no. Their problems are related to mine. Let me continue with the swimming pool analogy. About five years ago, our pool filled up. We had as many people in prison as we were intended to hold. Our outflow was steady. We released as many as we took in, or at least thereabouts.

BENNETT   The outflow is the parole group, right?

ALLEN   Yes, and the discharge group: those not yet paroled but released due to termination of sentence.

BENNETT But you control the outflow.

ALLEN Not hardly! The Corrections Department can't control either the inflow or the outflow. The criminal code and the sentencing judge control our intake, and the Parole Board and legislative restrictions on discharge control our releases.

BENNETT Oh. I think I'm beginning to get the picture.

ALLEN Every time the legislature passes a mandatory or determinant sentencing bill, they mess with the intake valve or the outflow valve or both. Ditto for every restriction on parole or time off for good behavior. We're caught in the middle. I can't control admissions, nor can I order releases without legislative authorization.

BENNETT What have you been able to do to adjust to the overflow?

ALLEN Well, I can't really let it overflow, can I? I wouldn't be Commissioner long if I let inmates get away from me. We have double-bunked our cells and converted some program space to sleeping space.

BENNETT Program space like classrooms and workshops?

ALLEN Right. We have also refitted some vacated mental health buildings for minimum security inmates. But these are stop gap measures.

BENNETT What you really need to do is to get rid of some of the prisoner overflow.

ALLEN Sometimes I try. Like I slow down the pickup of new inmates from local jails.

BENNETT I bet the sheriffs really love that!

ALLEN I'm sure that you've heard that they're after my head. The governor gets calls complaining about local jail backlog every day. One sheriff said he was going to bring his state inmates to a nearby prison, handcuff them to the fence, and leave.

BENNETT Do you think he'll do it?

ALLEN Nothing would surprise me at this point.

BENNETT So, that's how we come to the $100 million?

ALLEN That's it.

BENNETT There are no other options.

ALLEN I didn't say that. There are always options. Politics is all about options. But there aren't any options that don't have some monetary or political costs.

BENNETT Should the governor lobby for more liberalized sentences? Or more liberalized parole guidelines?

ALLEN Are you asking me my personal opinion?

BENNETT Yes, if that's fair.

ALLEN On or off the record?

BENNETT Any way it suits you, Commissioner.

ALLEN Well, Ms. Bennett, I don't think we can go on fantasizing that we can have it both ways. All this law-and-order rhetoric in political campaigns and in the legislature makes great headlines. But it doesn't get the job done when you get right down to it. Politicians who think you can dramatically increase prison populations and not substantially raise corrections budgets are just fooling themselves, or fooling somebody.

BENNETT So you think we're all being pretty irresponsible.

ALLEN I do. I think public officials play to the media. And the media are interested in slogans and melodrama. That's what sells newspapers.

BENNETT Ouch!

ALLEN You asked me what I thought.

BENNETT So what will happen if no corrective action is taken? What if the sentencing and release laws aren't changed or if new prisons aren't built.

ALLEN Already, inmates are sleeping in the halls. Some states have resorted to setting up tents on prison yards. Correctional officers are stretched to the breaking point. The few good sound institutions we have are being wrecked by overuse. It could all come apart.

BENNETT Like Attica or New Mexico?

ALLEN Yes. Or we could just slowly cave in with employee absenteeism and alcoholism, inmate suicides, reckless escape attempts, and so on.

BENNETT You don't paint a very pretty picture.

ALLEN We're living on borrowed time.

BENNETT What about the federal courts? Are they going to intervene?

ALLEN They already have. Most states are involved in litigation over prison conditions. Many of the unsanitary or unprofessional conditions that the courts are calling "cruel and unusual" are related to overcrowding.

BENNETT Well, the federal court sounds like a valuable ally.

ALLEN You could look at it that way, I suppose. But it makes me mad as hell to have someone telling me how to do my job. You'd think we were a bunch of stone age sadists to hear some of the lawyers and reformers talk.

BENNETT So, corrections should police itself?

ALLEN We try. The American Correctional Association has professional standards for prison operations, but they're voluntary. And, frankly, our low budgets and overcrowded conditions would keep us from meeting the standards right now.

BENNETT So court intervention is a good thing?

ALLEN Frankly, it may serve the greater public interest.

BENNETT Commissioner, if you could change one thing about the prison system today—with a snap of your fingers—what would it be?

ALLEN Well, it wouldn't be five new prisons.

BENNETT What, then?

ALLEN Maybe a really adequate community corrections program aimed at our youth.

BENNETT How would that help?

ALLEN It wouldn't help me here today. Later today I'll still have to argue for building adequate prisons, releasing the less dangerous offenders, and using adult probation more effectively on the front end of the system. But maybe the next commissioner or the next could preside over a more reasonable situation if we reached more youth today.

BENNETT So you take the long view.

ALLEN I guess so. There's no quick fix to today's prison crisis.

BENNETT Maybe "crisis" is an appropriate word for this situation.

ALLEN Not just political posturing?

BENNETT Maybe not.

ALLEN Well, thanks for at least letting me have my say.

BENNETT Thanks for your time, Commissioner Allen.

I left his office pretty depressed. It was a little after 8:00 a.m. and it was still raining. My day was going to be a long one. I had two other interviews, a staff meeting, and this write-up to do before 6:00 p.m. But at least I could get out and around town. Daniel Allen seemed as much a prisoner of his system as any inmate. How could he stand in there with all that pressure for 15 years? He's a tough little guy. I had to admit it: I liked him. But I still wouldn't have his job, not even for $100 million.

DISCUSSION QUESTIONS

1. What problem did Commissioner Allen share with Helen Bennett on the morning in question?
2. According to Commissioner Allen, what has caused the crisis facing his department?
3. How has the department responded to the population crisis? What other ways, options, or alternatives does it have?
4. To what degree is the population crisis determined or affected by other sectors of the criminal justice system? How do state penal code provisions enter into this?
5. Who should be sent to prison? What do you think of nonincarcerative penalties for criminal offenders? How do you think the public might respond?

SUGGESTED READING
"INTERVIEW WITH COMMISSIONER ALLEN"

Austin, James and Aaron David McVey
    1988   *The NCCD Prison Population Forecast: The Growing Imprisonment of
    America.* San Francisco, California: National Council on Crime and Delinquency.

    A concise analysis of prison population trends and an analysis of the potential consequences of
    escalating incarceration. Austin and McVey emphasize that the rate of imprisonment in the United
    States has increased by almost 800 percent since 1850 and provide more detailed statistical profiles
    of incarceration trends.

Blumstein, Alfred, Jacqueline Cohen, and Harold Miller
    1980   "Demographically Disaggregated Projections of Prison Populations." *Journal
    of Criminal Justice* 8: 1-25.

    An analysis of likely trends in prison populations by leading criminologists.

Clear, Todd R. and George F. Cole
    1986   *American Corrections.* Pacific Grove, California: Brooks/Cole.

    A current textbook on American corrections with specific attention to increases in prison populations
    in Chapter Nine.

Johnson, Robert
    1987   *Hard Times: Understanding and Reforming the Prison.* Pacific Grove
    California: Brooks/Cole.

    An introduction to the structure and organization of corrections with particular attention to efforts
    to remedy the most serious problems facing state prison systems.

Gaes, Gerald C.
    1985   "The Effects of Overcrowding in Prison." In Michael Tonry and Norval
    Morris, Editors. *Crime and Justice: An Annual Review of Research-*Volume 6.
    Chicago, Illinois: University of Chicago Press: 95-146.

    A comprehensive and critical review of research on the effects of prison overcrowding. Although
    Gaes acknowledges that prison crowding can be measured in a variety of objective ways, he points
    out that research does not establish many adverse effects. However, the author does note that
    researchers agree on the adverse effects of open bay dormitory arrangements.

Case Thirteen

Looking for State Prison

Wilbur Jenkins was a rather routine petty offender. His rap sheet listed several minor infractions and two DUIs. Although he did not represent a serious risk to the criminal justice system, he was one of those offenders whom courts sometimes watch out for. When he appeared before the Metro Superior Court for his third DUI, a burglary charge, and two minor infractions, Judge Dolores Burton expressed some concern. To be sure, Judge Burton had faced several more serious offenders. Metro Superior Court was situated in a large city in the northeast. With approximately 450,000 residents in the central city and an additional three million in surrounding counties, the metropolitan area had its share of crime and many of the more serious offenders passed through Burton's court on the way to the state prison system.

Jenkins had pled guilty to the DUI and the burglary. Forsaking even the appearance of a plea bargain, he told Judge Burton that he was serious about mending his ways. Furthermore, he asked if she would send him to one of the state's two trial "shock probation" units. Modeled after military "boot camp," these shock probation units were run from two of the state's county correctional institutions. Formerly part of the more independent county work camps, these correctional institutions now came under the jurisdiction of the centralized correctional system. Inmates sometimes worked for the local county government under contractual arrangements with the state, although those confined in the two shock probation units did not leave the confines of the institution.

Shock probation was being touted as a potentially effective deterrent. Specifically, it was designed to discourage petty offenders from pursuing a more serious line of crime. Wilbur Jenkins seemed to be the ideal prospect. At 25, he did not have any felony arrests prior to the current burglary charge, he was married, had some history of employment in construction, and seemed genuinely interested in reformation. Judge Burton thought that his request to try his 90 day sentence in shock probation was a reasonable option. The district attorney agreed, so Judge Burton ruled that Jenkins was to serve 90 days in the Mansfield Correctional Institution with a two-year probation term to follow. Sentenced on April 18, he was to be taken to Fairfield County Jail (Metro City was included in Fairfield County) to await a transfer to Mansfield. There inmates were forced to rise early and were subject to a rigorous physical exercise program and work details reminiscent of Paris Island, the tough training program for Marine recruits. Part of the program was designed to wear the inmates down and to force them to let go of whatever identity they brought with them to prison.

Jenkins was happy with his sentence and assured Judge Burton that she would not see him again. He promised that he would not only commit himself to the 90-day program at Mansfield, but that he would also complete his two-year probation term with no new offense, petty or otherwise. Judge Burton reminded him that his 90-day alcohol-free stay in Mansfield should convince him that he could live without booze. Furthermore, she warned him that if he did not successfully complete either the Mansfield program or his probation, he would wind up in the state prison at Dallas. Reputed to be a tough and unforgiving place, Jenkins and Burton both knew that if he wound up there, it would be over.

The Mansfield Correctional Institution was located some 75 miles from Metro City in a rather rural community. Local residents liked the institution and were grateful for the employment that it brought to the area. Furthermore, they enjoyed the notoriety that the experimental shock probation program brought. Heralded as an answer to both overcrowded prisons and an effective correctional system, the shock probation program seemed to offer something for everybody. The sentence of time served seemed to satisfy the more retributive aims of victims, while the rehabilitative character of the training program, albeit cast in military terms, seemed to satisfy those with a more treatment orientation. Furthermore, the possibility of deterrence struck a positive chord in virtually everyone. For the corrections department and the sentencing judge, the combination of short-term incarceration and probation helped to alleviate the overcrowded prison system.

Shock probation, however, was too popular with many of the state's trial judges. Record numbers of misdemeanor defendants and convicted felons were sent to Mansfield and its counterpart in Rochester in the southeast sector of the state. Each of the shock probation units could house 150 inmates, although staff preferred to work with less than a hundred. Since the program had been initiated two years ago, more and more offenders were being sentenced to the Mansfield and Rochester programs. When Judge Burton sentenced Jenkins to Mansfield, he was taken to the Fairfield County Jail to wait for a spot in the shock probation program. Little did Judge Burton or Jenkins realize at that time that the defendant would serve in excess of his 90-day sentence there.

Fairfield County Jail was a depressing place. It housed those charged with criminal offenses and those awaiting trial who were unable to make bond. Additionally, it housed convicted misdemeanants who were serving time for specific infractions and superior court prisoners waiting for transfers to any number of state institutions. In short, the population was considerably varied. Complicating the diversity in population and the varying levels of security each required was the fact that the jail was grossly overcrowded. In fact, inmates were currently working with a local attorney on filing a class action suit in federal court challenging the constitutional status of the jail's conditions. Such suits were not uncommon for both jails and prisons as any correctional authority could testify.

Jenkins was not happy at the prospect of any confinement in Fairfield's jail. He shared a cell designed for two inmates with four other men and had little opportunity for either exercise or work. Idle time was Jenkins' biggest complaint. The hours passed very slowly. Although he and his cellmates occasionally tried checkers or cards, they usually ended up quarreling. When Jenkins' wife, Betty, visited, she noted that he seemed very depressed. Although it had only been a week since he was brought to the jail, he told her he was worried that they would never get him to Mansfield. Grumbling about the jail, its conditions, and his cellmates, Wilbur told Betty that his guilty plea obviously hadn't helped much.

The days at Fairfield Jail passed by and, in short order, Wilbur counted 90 days. Looking at no one in particular, Jenkins observed that he had now served the 90 days time Burton had handed out and he was still locked up in this hellhole. The wing that housed Jenkins and his cellmates was designated as medium security. None of those housed there was awaiting transfer to state prison for violent crimes. In fact, most were eagerly waiting for a transfer to either the Mansfield or Rochester Programs. Frequently, they and their families viewed the program as a way out of crime. Certainly, some regarded the physical pressure of the shock probation's boot camp regime as preferable to the idle hours spent in cells or watching television. June 13th constituted Jenkins 96th day of confinement since sentencing. Jenkins figured someone should be able to do something. When his cell door was left ajar in the morning, he took his court papers, showed them to a secretary, and walked out. No one appeared to run after him since the secretary, a temporary replacement, thought the exit was legal and notified no one of Jenkins' departure.

Leaving the jail, Jenkins walked to a street near a thruway entrance ramp and hitched a ride to his in-law's house in one of the counties surrounding Metro City. His wife's parents, George and Susan Hendrix, told Wilbur that he should turn himself in to the authorities and explain his situation. Considering the 96 days Jenkins had already served in Fairfield Jail, they were convinced that the correctional officials would be sympathetic. Jenkins was not initially convinced and confided to his in-laws that he didn't think his 96 days in Fairfield County Jail counted for his 90-day sentence to shock probation. Furthermore, he said the jail conditions were terrible, he never had enough to eat, and he was bored to death.

Jenkins left his in-laws after telling them that he planned to hitch a ride to the Mansfield Correctional Institution and ask to be let into the shock probation program. Jenkins hitchhiked a ride to Storrs, 20 miles from the Mansfield Correctional Institution. After telling his story to the truck driver who gave him the lift, Jenkins decided to turn himself in to the nearest law enforcement authority. The truck driver agreed to take him to the Duchess County Sheriff where Jenkins turned himself in to a deputy sheriff. Tom Call, the deputy, listened as Jenkins outlined his story and told him to go home and wait for the state correctional authorities to pick him up for the Mansfield program. According to a later newspaper report, Call said that he didn't think Jenkins had escaped. "He told me he was sentenced to go to the shock unit at

Mansfield. So I told him, 'Go on home and wait. When your name comes up, they'll come and get you to.' I didn't think anything about him being an escapee because we have plenty of shock inmates working and waiting at home to be picked up."

Taking the deputy's advice, Jenkins left with the truck driver and went home. Thinking about the whole situation, he began to worry and decided to turn himself in yet a second time. Returning to the Duchess County Sheriff's office, he went over his situation but took pains to explain that he had walked out of the Fairfield County Jail. Although Jenkins never admitted to an escape—he insisted that someone had turned him loose— the Duchess sheriff locked him up and contacted the state correctional office.

The state correctional office was taken aback at the situation, particularly since they reported that a state van had gone to the Fairfield County Jail on June 13 to pick up Jenkins for the Mansfield shock Probation Program. According to the spokesperson for the Department of Corrections, Jenkins returned to his cell after breakfast and a jail guard forgot to lock the door behind him. The spokesperson did admit, however, that Jenkins had showed his papers to a jail secretary and that he walked out of that facility virtually unnoticed. Although that jail comes under the control of the county government, the state Department of Corrections seemed to be embarrassed that a state prisoner could escape so easily and that there was such a backlog of state prisoners at local jails. The press spokesperson, however, noted that the state's correctional system was operating at "crisis capacity," and took the opportunity to remind the reporter that the corrections department needed more resources to operate enough shock programs to meet the demand.

When queried about Jenkins' legal status, the corrections spokesperson indicated that his escape could jeopardize his chances of entering the shock probation program. Reviewing the state penal code provision pertaining to jail/prison escape, John England noted that the Fairfield County authorities could charge Jenkins with a felony. If convicted, he would not qualify for the shock probation program as it was designed for offenders between 18 and 25 who had never served prison time. Since a felony conviction potentially carries a prison term, it was possible that Jenkins would have to "do time" in a state prison, thus eliminating his qualification for shock probation. Noting that it was up to the Fairfield authorities to decide whether they wanted to prosecute Jenkins and, if prosecuted and convicted, up to the sentencing judge as to sentence (probation or prison), England observed that the general situation was, certainly, a "sorry affair."

DISCUSSION QUESTIONS

1. Is Wilbur Jenkins justified in leaving the Fairfield County Jail?
2. Who is responsible for the security in Jenkins' release from the Fairfield County Jail?
3. Do you think Jenkins served the sentence originally imposed by Judge Burton when he left the Fairfield facility?
4. What reasons justify the state's custody of Wilbur Jenkins before space opened up in the Mansfield shock probation system?
5. Should Jenkins be prosecuted for escape?
6. What kind of offenders should be incarcerated?
7. How is this case related to the preceding one?

SUGGESTED READING
"LOOKING FOR STATE PRISON"

Abt Associates
    1980   *American Prisons and Jails,* 5 volumes. Washington, D.C.: National Institute of Justice.

    A comprehensive assessment of contemporary corrections at the state and local levels.

Blumstein, Alfred
    1988   "Prison Populations: A System Out of Control?" In Michael Tonry and Norval Morris, Editors. *Crime and Justice: A Review of Research* - Volume 10. Chicago, Illinois: University of Chicago Press: 231-266.

    A review of the dramatic rise in prison populations in the past fifteen years and an analysis of factors contributing to that increase. Blumstein emphasizes that no single factor is responsible for escalating prison populations and outlines alternate strategies for its reduction or control.

Call, Jack E.
    1983   " Recent Case Law on Overcrowded Conditions of Confinement." *Federal Probation* (September): 32.

    A review and synthesis of the case law pertaining to prison conditions in the wake of escalating populations and overcrowding. This review is particularly useful since prison and jail overcrowding feature in the institutional reform litigation where federal courts maintain supervision of local jails and state prisons.

Hall, Andy
    1987   *Systemwide Strategy to Alleviate Jail Crowding.* Washington, DC.: National Institute of Justice.

    A summary of a National Institute of Justice research project designed to identify the causes of jail crowding and to propose potential solutions to the problem.

Mancini, Norma
    1988   *Our Crowded Jails: A National Plight.* Washington D.C.: Bureau of Justice Statistics.

    A short summary of the overcrowding in the nation's jails and a review of the consequences for the entire justice system. Mancini emphasizes that jail crowding is a pervasive problem and that improvements in information sharing and technical services are essential to any proposed solution.

Case Fourteen

I'll See You Monday

OCTOBER 28

In the hallway outside the hearing room at the State Administrative Services building the sparks were beginning to fly. "I don't understand how you guys get away with this. You claim that routine due process rules don't apply because this is an administrative hearing. The whole issue is Mr. Fowler's alleged unwillingness to submit to supervision. Yet, by your very own admission, you didn't even try to supervise him." Don Chapman was obviously irritated by what had transpired during the parole revocation hearing and used the confines of the narrow corridor to vent his anger. "If you had done your job, my client wouldn't be on his way back to prison."

For his part, Gary Skinner, a veteran field officer with the State Department of Probation and Parole and supervisor of parolee Cecil Fowler bit his tongue. He had been involved in this type of encounter before. "Well I have to tell you, Mr. Chapman, I think you're mistaken. I appreciate your desire to protect Cecil's rights, but the Parole Board sets the rules for parole in this state and they expect parolees to abide by them. All I can say is that I think I gave Cecil a break, and if he would have taken advantage of it and done what I told him to do, there wouldn't have been a problem. Further, parole is a privilege, not a right."

"Even a privilege can't be revoked without evidence," retorted Chapman.

Skinner remained calm, "How much evidence do you need that Cecil made no effort to register for parole, that's a violation of rule one. That's why he was arrested. That's why he's before the board today. And that's why he's headed back to jail."

"That doesn't wash and you know it," Chapman angrily asserted. "Mr. Fowler doesn't own a car, but even if he did, the parole board isn't going to let him drive it. He lives 45 miles out of town, way out in the country, how do you expect him to get to Jonesburg? Walk?"

Don Chapman paced the hallway during a moment of tense silence. Gary Skinner folded his hands behind him and leaned against the wall, wondering how much more of this he would have to endure. "Man, how long is it going to take that deputy to fetch my prisoner?" he thought to himself.

Chapman began anew. "The evidence I'm talking about is your testimony about the gun, Cecil's drinking, and his visiting in Jonesburg with his girlfriend. You don't know that any of that's true because you didn't hardly even go in the house, and you surely didn't stay long enough to gather any real evidence to support your allegations. But that's what the parole board responded to and you know it!" Chapman glared at Skinner, "In a court of law your hearsay evidence wouldn't have held up for two minutes. You could have gone out to the farm with the papers he needed to sign to register. Instead you went out there with the notion of playing cop, but you got cold feet and blew it."

By now Gary Skinner's patience was wearing thin. The only reason he was standing in the hall was because it was his responsibility to deliver Cecil Fowler to Central Correctional Institute so that Cecil could begin serving the remainder of his original prison sentence. Skinner had to wait for the sheriff's deputies (who staff the holding cell) to return Cecil Fowler to his custody. Skinner felt that Chapman was badgering him and that Chapman's comments were getting personal; intended, perhaps, to embarrass him in front of the other parole officers and passersby. Just then a heavily manacled Cecil Fowler was escorted into the corridor by a deputy. Skinner took custody of the prisoner and immediately headed for the elevator. On the ride down in the elevator, Gary Skinner could now muse, with some relief, about what a pain the encounter with Chapman had been.

Finally, Skinner turned toward Fowler. "Cecil, where'd you find that lawyer?"

"I don't know," responded Fowler almost inaudibly. "My aunt hired him."

Skinner paused to absorb the richer implications of Cecil's comment. As they departed from the elevator, Skinner turned once again to his prisoner. "Well, Cecil, you tell your aunt that she got her money's worth. Chapman's a pretty good little ol' country lawyer."

SEPTEMBER 19

Cecil Fowler had been released from incarceration on Monday. Gary Skinner expected Cecil to stop in, since Jonesburg, where the district field office was located, was on the route that Cecil would logically take on his way home. But Cecil did not have a reputation for being a paragon of logical behavior, thus Gary was not overly concerned by Cecil's failure to show up.

By Wednesday afternoon, however, Cecil still had not contacted Skinner, his supervising parole officer, and it was now apparent that this was not a good way for Cecil to begin his parole. Skinner became even more concerned after he called Fowler's former spouse. According to her, Cecil was actually in Jonesburg and had gotten into town by borrowing his cousin's pick-up truck. His ex-wife told Skinner that he was visiting with a girlfriend he had taken up with prior to going to prison.

Gary went to the girlfriend's address and spoke with the obviously intoxicated woman who answered the door. She acknowledged being a good acquaintance of Cecil Fowler, but denied that he had visited her apartment. Further, she claimed not to have seen Fowler since his release from prison. Gary left the apartment, but was particularly disturbed by the woman's demeanor. He couldn't legally search the apartment looking for Cecil because he didn't have a warrant for his arrest. But if Cecil was, or had been, in the apartment and had also been drinking, trouble was brewing. Cecil's long history of problems related to alcohol abuse made drinking a significant threat to his ability to succeed on parole. Fowler would have to be found, soon.

On Thursday morning, Skinner decided to drive out to Cecil's farm near Flint Ridge to find out what was going on. His specific concern was that Fowler had not checked in with him within the required 48 hour period subsequent to his release. He was also concerned that Cecil had started drinking again and was driving a motor vehicle; both of these were violations of Fowler's parole conditions. Further, Fowler's ex-wife had said that Cecil had taken a shotgun from his cousin at the same time he borrowed the truck. Possession of a firearm was strictly forbidden for persons under parole supervision.

Flint Ridge was about 45 miles from Jonesburg, so the drive out gave Gary Skinner some time to consider a strategy for dealing with Fowler. Skinner became familiar with Cecil Fowler's personality and criminal record through a series of pre-release interviews and background investigations, and through conversations with another parole officer who had supervised Fowler about three years earlier. He had no convictions for violent criminal offenses, but he often became bellicose and was capable of assaultive behavior when he had been drinking. Since Cecil lived alone on an isolated farm bequeathed to him by his parents, Skinner was especially concerned that he would drink and drive if he had both alcohol and transportation available to him. On his most recent prison term, Cecil had served 16 months of a five year sentence for driving under the influence of alcohol. Fowler had six prior convictions for DUI and had served a jail sentence on one of those previous convictions.

As he approached the house, Gary Skinner was surprised to see not only a pick-up parked in the driveway, but also a Ford station wagon. When he knocked on the front door of the house there was initially no answer. After a brief moment, a voice on the other side of the door inquired, "What do you want?" Skinner opened the door cautiously while announcing who he was and saying that he was looking for Cecil Fowler. When he was able to see in, Skinner saw Cecil Fowler standing next to an overstuffed chair at the far side of the room. In the chair was the female acquaintance Skinner had met the day before.

"I asked you what you want," Fowler said repeating his earlier question.

Skinner replied, "I want to know why you haven't been to Jonesburg to sign up for parole supervision."

Fowler shrugged his shoulders and looked out the window. "I ain't got no way to get there. And I ain't got a phone to call."

Reminding Fowler of the agreement reached in his pre-release interview, Skinner pointed out, "Both you and your aunt said she would drive you anywhere you needed to go."

"I ain't going to have her do that," retorted Fowler.

Skinner ventured a little farther inside the front door so that he could get a better look at Cecil and his friend. He noticed that Cecil's female visitor was blurry-eyed and visibly agitated. For his part, Cecil too did not appear to be in very good shape. Gary Skinner detected a strong odor of alcohol in the living room. Cecil Fowler's comportment conveyed the distinct impression that he had had a good deal to drink even though it was only 10:00 in the morning.

"Cecil, have you been drinking this morning?" inquired Skinner. "Naw," Fowler answered setting his eyes and clenching his teeth. "But even if I had, this is my house and what I do here ain't your concern." Cecil's tone was surly, yet stuporous and charged with hollow truculence.

Nevertheless, Gary Skinner continued to probe. "Cecil, you know that your failure to report to me within 48 hours of your release from Central Correctional constitutes a violation of the terms of your parole. If you've been drinking, and I think that you have been, that too is a parole violation. I understand that you've been over to your cousin's and picked up a rifle that you have here in the house. Any truth to that?"

"I got a gun," snarled Fowler, "but it ain't here, it's at my cousin's."

"You mind if I look around the house a little bit, Cecil?" asked Skinner.

Cecil responded belligerently, "I think you had best stay where you're at." Sensing that the utility of his visit was nearing an end, Skinner opened a copy of Cecil Fowler's parole contract, handed it to him, and proceeded to read aloud each of its fourteen conditions. After each point Skinner paused to ask Cecil if he understood the point and if he intended to honor it.

With ritual consistency Fowler would brace himself and reply obstinately, "Naw, I ain't goin' do that."

Exasperated, Gary Skinner closed his notebook and headed toward the door. As he reached the door, he turned toward Fowler and said flatly, ". . . 9:00 Monday morning. I'll see you Monday morning in my office. If not, I'll be back with a warrant for your arrest Monday afternoon." Having said this, Skinner left the house and returned to the district field office in Jonesburg.

EPILOGUE

Cecil Fowler ordered two Whoppers, an order of fries, and a chocolate shake at Burger King. It was 1:45 p.m., the lunch hour had passed, but Gary indicated to Cecil that the state wanted Gary to make sure that Cecil did not miss lunch. Even though he could have seen to it that Cecil was fed a late lunch at Central Correctional Institute, he knew that the state would reimburse him if he bought something for Cecil from a commercial restaurant.

"This is pretty good stuff," Cecil exclaimed. "I reckon I ain't goin' to be seeing much good to eat for a spell."

"I suppose not," Skinner rejoined.

By 2:30 p.m., Gary Skinner and Cecil Fowler were parting company in the inmate reception area at Central Correctional. "You take care, Cecil; stay out of trouble. I imagine I'll be seeing you again in a few months."

In a manner that was a bit incongruous given his situation, Cecil responded with a broad grin, "I 'preciate the lunch. Ya'll take care too." With that, Gary Skinner returned to his car and started back for Jonesburg.

On the trip home, Gary and his partner (parole board regulations require that whenever possible two officers be assigned to transport parolees who are under arrest) exchanged thoughts about the day's events. "You know, Gary, Fowler sure was in a good mood when we dropped him off. I think feeding him lunch was probably a pretty good idea, don't you?"

"Right," Skinner replied. "With the hearing and all, I think ol' Cecil had been roughed up about enough for one day. We're going to see him again, soon. You've got to leave a guy with his dignity intact, or you can pretty much expect that you're going to have to wrestle with a bear when he gets out again."

Some time passed as both parole officers enjoyed the fall colors of the countryside. Then Skinner opened up, "Getting back to this dignity thing, that's what really gripes me about Fowler's lawyer. He gets on my case about how I handled the situation at Cecil's farm. Man, that guy doesn't realize how close I came to having to fight Cecil out there 40 miles in the woods. You back a parolee into a corner on his own turf, you might just wind up forcing him into a position where he has to save face in front of his family, running buddies, girlfriend, whomever."

Skinner paused for a moment to gather his thoughts. "I get a little tired of going to revocation hearings only to be depicted as the bad guy or, in this case, an inept bureaucrat. My first responsibility is to public safety, to protect people and property. Next, I'm going to take care of me. This job just plain doesn't pay enough for me to put my neck on the line every time I turn around. As you well know, I don't have much use for this community-based treatment stuff. How are you going to 'treat' Cecil Fowler? Nevertheless, we've gotta remember that even hard core screw-ups have a need to protect their dignity and sense of self-respect. You forget that and you're going to be fightin' them every time you turn around."

"Amen," Skinner's partner remarked as he nodded approvingly and resumed gazing out the window.

DISCUSSION QUESTIONS

1. If you were in Gary Skinner's position, how would you have handled the encounter with Don Chapman?
2. Do you agree with the conclusion that Don Chapman is "a pretty good little ol' country lawyer?"
3. From the evidence in the case, how would you describe Gary Skinner's style of parole supervision? Do you think this is an appropriate approach?
4. Are Cecil Fowler's "problems" confined to his apparent alcohol abuse? What other factors might be considered to explain his behavior?
5. What is the proper role of discretion in the administration of justice? Do you think Cecil Fowler's civil rights were violated in the parole revocation hearing?

SUGGESTED READING
"I'LL SEE YOU MONDAY"

Barkin, Eugene
  1979   "Legal Issues Facing Parole." *Crime and Delinquency.* 25: 219-235.

  This article deals with the difficulty parole boards encounter in making parole revocation proceedings constitutionally valid. Barkin points out that questions of due process arise at a number of junctures in the revocation process including the admissibility of testimony, time requirements for scheduling hearings, and the liability of parole boards for criminal acts committed by persons on parole.

Clear, Todd R. and Vincent O'Leary
  1983   *Controlling the Offender in the Community.* Lexington, MA: Lexington Books.

  Clear and O'Leary define the goal of this book to be the identification of a program for the reform of case supervision in community-based corrections. The authors develop the notion of "risk control" in the community organized around three principles: controlling (minimizing) the degree of coercive social control in community corrections, adherence to high standards of due process, and reaffirmation of the importance of change as a systemic dimension of criminal justice policy.

Moseley, William H.
  1977   "Parole: How Is It Working?" *Journal of Criminal Justice.* 3: 185-203.

  This article provides comparative data on the success of parole in relation to other methods of releasing offenders from incarceration. The principle finding of the paper is that parolees tend to be more successful in their communities than individuals who are released through other procedures.

Sklar, Robert
  1964   "Law and Practice in Probation and Parole Revocation Hearings." *Journal of Criminal Law, Criminology, and Police Science.* 55: 175-198.

  Sklar's paper provides a comprehensive and highly useful inventory of legal issues related to parole revocation processes. Although dated, the article contains information that represents a baseline for the study of evolving standards of due process in revocation hearings.

Star, Deborah and John E. Berecochea
  1984   "Rationalizing the Conditions of Parole." pp.286- 305 in R.M. Carter, D. Glaser, and L.T. Wilkins (eds.) *Probation, Parole, and Community Corrections.* New York: John Wiley & Sons.

  The conditions of parole placed on an ex-offender can be expansive. The authors report the results of a California study of patterns of parole rule violation. The goal of the study was to find ways of streamlining parole rules without increasing the risk of parole failure.

Takagi, Paul and James Robison
  1969   "The Parole Violator: An Organizational Reject."*Journal of Research in Crime and Delinquency.* 6: 78-86.

  Parole violation depends not only on the behavior of parolees but also on the tolerance limits that parole officers impose on the behavior of their clients. The authors presented a set of hypothetical cases to a sample of parole officers. These cases depicted behaviors that could lead to parole revocation depending on the judgment of the parole officer. The research documents the wide range of variability in officers' views regarding the revocability of parole based on this set of hypothetical cases.

Case Fifteen

I Just Need the Data

BACKGROUND

Trudy Graham was a doctoral student in sociology at State University. After completing her preliminary examinations, she started her dissertation research. Trudy had long been concerned about both the crime and law relating to rape. After considerable thought, she decided to study rape offenders. Specifically, she wanted to see if there were any common features in their background or if they shared some similar perspectives about women and/or sex. Of course, Trudy realized that she had to talk to prison inmates. There simply was no other way she could address the questions she had posed.

After some preliminary telephone calls to the state's Corrections Department, Trudy scheduled an appointment with that agency's research head. Bob Fox was a personable, intelligent young man. With extensive graduate study in both law and social science, he had served as the department's research division head for about two years. In that position Bob supervised all the agency's in-house research. This frequently took two forms: preparing short papers on questions raised by legislators and other public figures and working on more extensive research projects for the commissioner. In addition, Bob was in charge of the agency's research proposal review board.

Since the late 1960s a variety of people routinely asked the agency for information, specifically access to either its records or permission to interview agency employees or inmates. During their busiest time, Bob estimated that his office received 10 to 12 such requests each week. At first the Corrections Department simply relied on Bob's judgment. If the request focused on some controversial data or involved many staff work hours, Bob consulted with the commissioner. As the requests for data access increased, however, and concerns about inmate and staff privacy intensified, the commissioner decided that a more formal approach was needed to screen requests for access to the departments records, staff, or inmates.

With Bob's help, the commissioner set up a review board. The board consisted of five members: representatives from the agency's records and operations divisions, a staff social scientist, an external expert (e.g., lawyer or professor), and the head of the research office. This board met and outlined the procedures they would follow when faced with research proposals. In the process they decided on the following. First, all requests had to be made in writing. Second, the researcher not only had to detail the question and topic, but also had to establish its importance and timeliness. Additionally, the researcher had to specify whether he/she wanted to conduct the research in the agency or to retrieve information that would be recorded elsewhere. In either instance, the researcher had to specify the cost to the agency, specifically, what kind of assistance or cooperation was needed. Finally, the researcher had to offer some assurance that the research posed no risk or undue inconvenience to the department's staff or inmates.

Trudy Graham appreciated these instructions and proceeded to draft a proposal for the review board. She reviewed the literature on rape and commented on the etiological controversies that she wanted to examine. Specifically, she emphasized that she was interested in learning more about rape offenders, their backgrounds, and their perspectives/attitudes toward women. To do this, Trudy needed two things from the Department of Corrections: (1) she needed a list of inmates convicted and imprisoned for rape and (2) permission to interview in the prison. The former required some assistance from the agency's research staff, while the latter could not be carried out without the cooperation of prison administrators and staff.

The review board was concerned about Trudy's request. First, they were generally disinclined to grant access of any kind. Requests for agency assistance in external research were so common that if the board routinely approved the majority, the pressures on both central office staff and the institutions themselves would be substantial. Second, the board was concerned about the nature and sensitivity of the research in question. Finally, there were concerns that could most appropriately be described as political.

Long before Trudy had filed her proposal, a professor from State University had asked for and been granted access to the agency's inmates' files. Looking at the relationship between race and felony sentencing, this researcher concluded that the state's system was blatantly discriminatory. These findings were well publicized in the popular press and the scholar in question had started to serve as an expert witness in appellate reviews of sentencing disparity. Although the research in question did not cast any unfavorable light on the Corrections Department, the commissioner and his staff felt as though they were under attack. Furthermore, they were indirectly affected by the appellate litigation as the appeals entailed considerable cost to the state.

When Trudy's proposal came to the board, then, their typical reluctance was intensified and Trudy faced substantial opposition. When the board met to learn more about her project, they asked several questions about the sensitivity of the offense and the inmates' probable reluctance to cooperate in interviews. Some voiced concern for Trudy's safety. "These guys don' t exactly like women," one board member observed, while others suggested that such interviews would be difficult to set up in the confines of the maximum security prison. The lawyer on the panel expressed the most vehement reservations. "I don't see how your research outweighs the assault on the inmates' privacy. You want to delve into their family lives, review all the dark spots in their childhood, and get them to 'open up.' That's asking a lot—especially from rape offenders. Don't you think they might be just a little sensitive to your project."

Trudy was disheartened when she left the meeting. Although she did not expect to get the agency's permission without some effort, she didn't anticipate the resistance she met. "I won't go to the press with any lurid stories, and I'll certainly try not to embarrass the inmates. I just need the data," she emphasized. Talking things over with her faculty supervisor, she concluded that perhaps she should start looking for another dissertation topic. Her supervisor agreed and observed that he had warned her that agency permission might be very difficult.

Two weeks later Trudy received an official notice from the Corrections Review Board. Her proposal had been rejected; in short, she would not be given a list of the inmates imprisoned for rape and she could not conduct interviews with those offenders in prison. The review board took pains to assure Trudy that they thought her proposal was sound—from a scientific point of view. However, the political and administrative costs were far too substantial and outweighed the scholarly merit of her proposed study. In the letter the board noted that prison interviews with rape offenders and extensive probing of their personal histories carried far too much of a risk of an invasion of privacy. Furthermore, they emphasized that there would be substantial costs to the agency itself, especially the inconvenience of setting up individual interviews in a maximum security prison.

After some weeks of reflection, Trudy admitted that she should not have been surprised with the agency's decision. She had taken a course on correctional law in graduate school and recalled the many hours she had spent reviewing the regulations relating to privacy. Specifically, Trudy remembered that this concern with privacy of criminal justice information was rather recent. After the establishment of the Law Enforcement Assistance Administration in 1969, federal monies were used to computerize and centralize criminal justice information. Federal authorities, however, were concerned lest the resulting more convenient and, hopefully, comprehensive, data files be issued. Early in 1973 the National Advisory Commission on Criminal Justice Standards and Goals urged each state to " . . . adopt enabling legislation for protection of security and privacy of criminal justice information systems." Shortly after, in 1973 the Crime Control Act amended the earlier 1968 legislation that set up LEAA and required that "information systems developed with federal funds be protected by measures to insure the privacy and security of criminal justice information." This amendment was given an additional boost in 1974 when the Federal Privacy Act was passed, thus intensifying the need to receive permission from the individuals on whom the information is kept.

Trudy thought she had complied with all these guidelines and with the specific procedures set out by the state and its Corrections Department. Although she would not ask each inmate to give permission for his rape history to be shared with her, she emphasized that she would make sure that those who participated in the interviews did so voluntarily. In fact, she drafted consent forms and included these in her request to the Research Review Board. Additionally, she explained that no inmate would be forced or even encouraged to participate in her research.

Several weeks after she received the agency's formal notice of refusal, Trudy was still bothered by her failure to gain access to the information and inmates she needed for her dissertation research. Although she agreed with her major professor on the need to find another topic, she lamented to friends that the denial didn't seem fair. "I just needed the data," she repeated. "I wasn't going to run to the papers or testify in trials."

DISCUSSION QUESTIONS

1. Is the state justified in screening research proposals for information access?
2. What interests do you think dominate the state's concern in Trudy Graham's case?
3. Could Trudy Graham have presented her request in a potentially more successful fashion?
4. Does Trudy Graham have any rights in this situation?
5. Should Trudy Graham and other researchers obtain consent from inmates when asking for access to their files?
6. What is more compelling, Trudy Graham's research interest/right to information *or* the privacy invoked by the state?
7. Do prison inmates have any privacy claims?

SUGGESTED READING
"I JUST NEED THE DATA"

Pelair, Robert R.
  1985   *Public Access to Criminal History and Record Information.* Washington, D.C.: U.S. Department of Justice.
    A review of the extent to which criminal history information is open to the public and an analysis of the appropriateness of such access. The author argues that criminal history information is more readily available now than in the past but that legal regulations limit access.

Cooper, Gary R. and Robert R. Belair
  1979   *Privacy and Security of Criminal History Information.* Washington D.C.: Bureau of Justice Statistics.
    A concise consideration of a variety of questions relating to the privacy and security of criminal records. Cooper and Belair address general issues of criminal justice information law and policy, and speak to the particular demands placed on the system by the news media.

Henshel, Richard

> 1980   "Political and Ethical Considerations of Evaluative Research." In Susette M. Talarico, Editor. *Criminal Justice Research: Approaches, Problems, and Policy.* Cincinnati, Ohio: Anderson Publishing Company: 231-236.

> Originally published in Henshel's book, *Reacting to Social Problems* in 1976, this piece offers a thorough but concise analysis of the political and ethical dimensions of a considerable portion of social science research. Particularly germane to criminal justice is Henshel's remarks on the difficulty of obtaining research support and research access.

Schlesinger, Steven R. et al.

> 1988   *Open v. Confidential Records: Proceedings of a BJS/SEARCH Conference.* Washington, D.C.: U.S. Department of Justice.

> Statements on confidentiality issues by a variety of public authorities, academics, and interest group/ professional association staff.

> 1988   Compendium of State Privacy and Security Legislation. Washington D.C.: U.S. Department of Justice.

> Sixth report in a series of compendia of state law related to the collection and use of criminal history information and records. Summary and classification tables are especially useful reference sources.

PART FOUR
Special Topics

Introduction

Criminal Justice covers so many disparate topics and is guided by an equally diverse set of policies that there are endless special topics that could be considered in a casebook such as this. In this section, however, we focus on those issues that relate to two basic concerns: the causes of criminality and the purposes ascribed for criminal law. In the strict sense criminology encompasses issues related to the etiology of crime, while criminal justice deals with the purposes of the criminal sanction. Since both issues are usually introduced in criminal justice courses, however, we offer cases that illustrate points related to both.

The first case, *Arrest Me, Arrest Me,* looks at the relationship between deviance and crime. In this story, a police officer is confronted by a man whose behavior is at least deviant. However, some are tempted to define his actions and demeanor in more criminal terms. Whether defined as criminal or deviant, the behavior outlined in the case causes considerable difficulty for the police officer in question and illustrates the fact that police are often asked to deal with both criminals and social misfits.

The second case, *Her First Job,* focuses on a rather routine instance of white-collar crime, specifically employee theft. The story of a department store clerk not only illustrates a particular type of criminality but also explores different theories about the causes of crime. Of potential application are criminological theories related to differential association and social learning. How they apply to the case at hand and to other types of criminal behavior is an issue for the reader to decide.

The third case, *I Want My Property Returned,* looks at the relationship between the victim and the offender, and at the different objectives people ascribe for criminal law. As exemplified in the case title, the victim of this nonviolent property crime is only interested in getting his belongings back. Of little concern is the need for public censure or penalty. In this case, the victim's particular objective limits the response the criminal justice system can make and illustrates the implications of different criminal sanction priorities. How nonrestitutive penalties (e.g., deterrent, rehabilitative, incapacitative, or even retributive) could be applied is left to the reader to decide.

Domestic violence poses substantial challenges and problems to criminal law and the justice system. Of particular concern are the obstacles to the enforcement of the law and the possibility that individuals will take the law into their own hands when either the participants do not look for formal dispute resolution or the law doesn't address the problem. *Don't Hurt My Mama* details a particular instance of domestic violence and the efforts one child took to protect his mother from an abusive boyfriend. The case prompts a discussion of the role and place of vengeance in criminal law and other issues related to criminal prosecution. Included in the latter are self-defense and extensions of the battered wife syndrome. Because of this last dimension, the case could also be examined in a discussion of criminal court operations.

The final case, *Honest John,* combines issues related to both the etiology of crime and the purposes of criminal law. In this story, a man is being victimized and seeks some official response. As the case outlines, however, the victim is, at some level, a party to his own victimization. This complicates the clear application of criminal law and the degree to which the criminal justice system can respond to the crime at hand. As in so many criminal cases, *Honest John* illustrates the complicated relationship that sometimes exists between offender and victim. How this complexity affects the application of criminal law and the effectiveness of the criminal justice system is left to the reader to consider.

The following chart outlines each of these five cases and points to the concepts and issues illustrated in each. The reader is again asked to consider how these issues are reflected in the five stories and to respond to the problem at hand or the resolution described. In the process, it is the authors' hope that the cases will help students to appreciate the complexity of crime and criminal law, and to develop the analytical skills necessary for an informed and critical appraisal of the criminal justice system.

PART FOUR: SPECIAL TOPICS

Case Title	Central Subject	Concepts/Issues
Arrest Me, Arrest Me	police contact with social misfit	deviance and criminality service demands on police police roles
Her First Job	employee theft	white collar criminality differential association and social learning theories techniques of neutralization
I Want My Property Returned	property victimization	victim-offender relationship victim reluctance to testify purpose of criminal sanction limits of the criminal justice system
Don't Hurt My Mama	domestic violence	violence among family members handgun availability and use vengeance and justice battered wife syndrome
Honest John	restitution	victim reluctance to press charges restitution and criminal justice limits on prosecutorial power

Case Sixteen

Arrest Me, Arrest Me

PART ONE

Abe Anderson was working as a janitor at Wade Thermodynamic Engineering Corporation at the time of his first encounter with the officers of the 17th precinct. Wade Thermodynamics designed and manufactured high technology thermodynamic controls for jet engines and rockets. Anderson belonged to a cleaning crew assigned to the offices that housed the corporation's professional and managerial staff. Abe, in his own way, was flattered that the plant managers had seen fit to assign him to these high status environs. He assumed that this decision was based not on manpower needs, but rather on an appreciation of his chic demeanor and suave interpersonal style—assets he was sure made him especially valuable to the "big boys."

In point of fact, "chic" and "suave" were hardly the words most people would use to describe Abe Anderson. Standing 6' 3' and weighing 150 pounds, Anderson was cast more in the likeness of a scarecrow than in the image of virility incarnate. Though neither physically deformed nor clinically mentally ill, the limitedness of his cognitive ability was obvious to everyone. The major reflection of this was conveyed in his tendency toward caddishness in social encounters. He mistook for erudition what others perceived as a childish fascination with off-color remarks and risque humor. When Abe thought he was being clever and witty, those around him often thought of him as gross and disgusting.

Among his more deviant behaviors, Anderson entertained the misperception that "girls" liked to be "hugged." This is what initially brought him to the attention of the officers of the 17th precinct and ultimately cost him his job. On at least three occasions, he was suspected of harassing female employees of Wade Thermodynamics by making unwelcomed sexual advances. These advances, though juvenile, were sufficiently annoying to lead to police investigations and, finally, to Abe's arrest.

Since Anderson was not considered to be a serious physical threat to female employees—even his most offensive behavior was perceived more as "jerkishness" than "criminal"—the charges against him were dropped with the understanding that he would terminate his employment at Wade and agree to keep off corporate property. Although he desisted from further episodes of sexual harassment, Anderson was subsequently picked up several times in and around the Wade offices on suspicion of criminal trespass.

Abe Anderson's problems with the law did not begin with the trouble he caused at Wade Thermodynamics. He had a long rap sheet filled with arrests for petty crimes including shoplifting, simple larceny, and past incidents of criminal trespass in other parts of the city. Some of his shopliftings were further evidence of his simplemindedness. It was not beyond Anderson to steal food from grocery stores, and begin to consume his loot while perched on the curb outside the store. Abe, on occasion, attributed these thefts to hunger, though at the time, there was not enough known about his background to place much credence in these accounts.

Abe Anderson was, then, no stranger to the 17th Precinct station house. This visit, however, was a little different from previous ones; this time he entered the station through the front door, unescorted by an arresting officer. Abe had a plan in mind.

As he entered the waiting area, Abe paused momentarily to gain his bearings. He then sneaked past the information desk toward the administration section. Seeing only clerks, typists, and other workers in civilian attire, he concluded that this was not where he wanted to be. He, after all, was looking for a cop. Turning in the direction opposite the administration section, Abe caught sight of a large "picture window" that provided a view of the precinct communication center. Through the window he could see a number of people in uniforms who looked to him to be just like the kind of folks he wanted to see.

Even though the communication center was strictly off-limits to unauthorized personnel, Abe entered the area ignoring the "off-limits" sign posted on the door. He stood just inside the door until he caught the eye of a dispatcher. Abe's dress and ambience (he had been several days without a change of clothes) made him immediately recognizable as an uninvited guest.

"Say, pal, you're not supposed to be in here," observed a dispatcher. "Whom are you looking for?"

"I'm looking for a cop," Anderson replied.

The dispatcher, perturbed by the distraction caused by the intruder, responded sarcastically, "Great! You've come to the right place. I'm a cop. Now, what do you want?"

Reassured, Abe approached the dispatcher and voiced his request. "Arrest me," he commanded.

"Do what?"

As if to clarify the situation, Abe repeated himself with elaboration, "Arrest me. I ain't s'pose to be here, so arrest me."

"Oh, boy," the dispatcher thought to himself. "I've got a live one here!"

"Just hold it right there," instructed the dispatcher as he turned his radio pod over to the control of another dispatcher. "You come with me and we'll get you squared away. How will that be little buddy?"

Satisfied that his demand would be honored, Abe nodded and stood by patiently.

Detective Joe Mitchell's day had not been going well. It was his special misfortune to be passing in the hall as the dispatcher escorted Abe Anderson from the communication center. In his office, Mitchell studied the emptiness of Anderson's frozen smile while trying to absorb the logic of such a strange request. There was something about Anderson that was familiar.

"I've seen you around here before, haven't I?" Mitchell inquired.

"Yup!" Abe replied.

"You're the guy who can't keep his hands off the ladies. Isn't that right?"

Anderson responded, "I like pretty girls. Jus' trying to be friendly."

"Have you been staying out of those office buildings like you've been told to do?" Mitchell asked.

"Yup!" said Abe.

Mitchell continued, "So now you're going to start pestering us. Is that the idea?"

"Nope . . . jus' wanta go to jail," replied Abe.

"You're aware, aren't you, that most people aren't quite so eager to get locked up?" inquired Mitchell.

"Yup!" said Abe.

Unhumored by Anderson's inane self-assurance, Mitchell snapped, "What's wrong with you, man?"

Anderson's features took on a sober and more fretful appearance, "I'm hungry, that's all."

Mitchell paused to consider Anderson's response. He was well aware of cases where street people, tramps and the like, would start just enough trouble to get themselves locked up for a night; this strategy had the dual advantage of securing a warm place to sleep and a couple of free meals. Most of these people, however, would have contact with the precinct once or twice and then move on. Further, Mitchell couldn't think of any cases where a person actually showed up at the station "volunteering" for arrest. While Mitchell recognized that as a police detective Abe Anderson was not his problem, he also understood that Anderson was not about to leave on his own initiative.

Mitchell continued his line of questioning by asking Anderson how long it had been since he had eaten.

"Long time," Anderson rejoined. "'Bout two days."

"And where are you staying now?" Mitchell inquired.

"Here and there," he said.

"Do you have any family in town?" asked Mitchell.

"Yup, my mama and sister both live here, but they mad at me and ain't neither one of 'em goin' to let me in their houses." Mitchell again considered the situation. While he was no "bleeding heart," he was also not immune to the misery that often manifested itself in the 17th Precinct. It would certainly be easy enough to arrest Anderson and have him taken to the county jail, but Mitchell sensed that this would be, at best, a short-term and fairly unprofessional approach to the problem. Mitchell sought a more permanent solution to the problems of Mr. Abraham Anderson.

Joe Mitchell debated what to do. He wondered whether the situation called for law enforcement, social work, or both. His intuition told him that Anderson's behavior stemmed from problems much more deeply rooted than his occasional brushes with the law. Over time, Mitchell arrived at the conclusion that at 34 years of age Abe was a perfect specimen of human social pathology. Mitchell discovered that Anderson was the second oldest in a family of five children. Abe's father had never adequately provided for the family and finally abandoned them shortly after the youngest child had been born. Because of his retardation, Anderson had been dependent on his mother and one of his sisters throughout his entire life. In recent years, his mother had become increasingly unable to provide for him because of her failing health. Abe's sister became disgusted with him after he had gotten into trouble at work. In her opinion, even his limited mental ability did not excuse such asinine behavior. She was now to the point that she forbade Abe to come to her house at all out of fear that he might harm her children. As sorry as she felt about the situation, Abe would just have to learn to fend for himself.

This became a lesson that Anderson would have difficulty learning. His childishness was not limited to a naive view of the dynamics of social interaction. His dependency on his mother and his sister had left him without the foggiest notion of how to survive independently. In the weeks after he lost his job, Abe faced ongoing problems with food and shelter; as he wandered aimlessly about he was, for the first time in his life, literally on his own. The best adaptation he had made—one that was proving to be highly satisfactory from his perspective—was to hang around the buildings at Wade Thermodynamics until he was arrested for trespassing. These arrests typically landed him in jail and thus temporarily provided him with a warm bed and a hot meal. So attractive had this strategy become, Abe concluded that he should go directly to the police station so as to shorten the time needed to transport him to the county jail.

Detective Mitchell checked with the watch commander to see if he had any suggestions on what to do with Abe Anderson. Major Hines was not much help. He agreed that jail was not the place to dispose of Anderson, but beyond that he simply instructed Mitchell to "handle it." As a reasonable alternative to jail, Mitchell decided to show Abe how to find his way to the Wandering Paraclete Holy Light Mission down by Warehouse Row. Although "the Row" as it was known, lay outside the 17th Precinct, it was not far from Anderson's old neighborhood and it was clearly a facility that specialized in problems such as those that confronted Abe. Here he would be able to get something to eat and have a temporary place to stay. Further, the mission staff would try to assist Anderson in finding work and a permanent residence. As Mitchell parted company with his charge in the lobby of the mission, he reminded Abe that if nothing else, the mission offered a far better place for him to go when he was down on his luck than reporting to the precinct station with "arrest me, arrest me," on his mind. Mitchell hoped that this would be the last he would see of Abe Anderson.

PART TWO

Joe Mitchell tried to contemplate what life must be like at the Torrance County Jail. Why, he asked himself, did Abe Anderson find this generally disgusting place to be so attractive? While a good answer was not forthcoming, Mitchell remained painfully aware that, in Abe's eyes, jail was the place to be. Anderson had presented himself at the 17th Precinct station house on no less than six occasions in the short time since Mitchell had taken him to the Wandering Paraclete Mission. On each visit Abe would beg to go to jail only to be turned down and ultimately driven to the Mission and dropped off.

Mitchell was annoyed, irked, and genuinely perplexed by Anderson's nuisance behavior. He was annoyed because each encounter caused him to lose precious time that should be devoted to the investigation of criminal cases. He was irked because he knew that police administrators in the precinct were not interested in his "petty" problems. Also, the other detectives were teasing him about becoming Anderson's "case worker" and, worse yet, his "chauffeur." He was perplexed because the State Department of Social Welfare and Mental Hygiene did not consider "able-bodied," sane males to be their responsibility. Further, the mission staff would gladly attend to Abe's needs, but only when he came to them. And finally, Abe for his part seemed incapable of any independent judgment or action to protect his own physical well-being.

"Say Joe," announced Detective Scott, "the chowderhead is here to see you."

"Oh #*&!, " exclaimed Mitchell. "Him again?"

Mitchell confronted Anderson before he even entered the room. "Let me guess. You wanna' go to jail?" Mitchell inquired as he greeted Anderson in the hall outside the detective's offices.

"Yup," replied Abe.

"No way," Mitchell retorted. "If you need help, you know where to go—so hit the road."

"You gotta drive me." Abe responded.

"No, we're not going to do that anymore. How did you get here, Abe?"

"Walked." Mitchell rejoined, "If you can walk here, you can walk there."

"But I afraid I get loss if I do that," Abe pleaded.

Mitchell opened the door to his office, but paused before he entered. "Great! If that happens then I might not have to fool with you again. So long Abe. Good-bye and good luck. Now get!"

Closing the door to his office he left Anderson standing in the hallway of the station house.

Mitchell offered his thoughts to Detective Scott. "Social junk," he exclaimed. "That's what they call these guys in the textbooks."

"Garbage need collecting? Refuse? Social junk?" Scott proffered mockingly. "Call Joe Mitchell at the 17th Precinct, 555-3000 for routine collection, 911 for emergencies."

DISCUSSION QUESTIONS

1. What are Abe Anderson's socially discreditable attributes? What elements of his conduct are directly related to deviant behavior? What deviant statuses does he possess? What is the relationship between his "deviance," and Abe as a "deviant?"

2. Identify the diverse mechanisms of social control that have been imposed on Anderson within the story. In the aggregate, do these mechanisms tend to reduce or increase the deviance of Abe Anderson?

3. Evaluate Detective Mitchell's handling of this case. Are there elements in Anderson's background that would have made his arrest justifiable? Is Abe dangerous? Why does Mitchell think arresting Anderson would be "unprofessional?" What are the "pros" and "cons" of Mitchell's actions?

4. What are the implications of Abe Anderson's behavior for the routine activities of people working in the criminal justice system? If Detective Mitchell really believes that Anderson is "not his problem," why does he invest valuable police time in dealing with Anderson's situation? Is Mitchell's conduct simply a response to the immediate situation, or does he define his professional responsibilities fairly broadly?

5. Abe Anderson does not mind going to jail; in fact, he relishes it. Do you think there are many people like him in society? If you do, what are the implications of this for the use of the criminal justice system as a social control institution?

SUGGESTED READING
"ARREST ME, ARREST ME"

Aulette, Judy and Albert Aulette
    1987 "Police Harrassment of the Homeless: The Political Purpose of the Criminalization of Homelessness. *Humanity and Society.* 11: 244-256.

    The treatment accorded homeless people does not always equal the tolerance of Abe Anderson shown by Detective Mitchell. The Aulette and Aulette article examines special strategies that some communities have used to harass and intimidate homeless persons, and to criminalize homelessness. The essay deals with how the enforcement of crimes such as trespassing, loitering, and panhandling can be specifically directed toward the homeless.

Barsuk, Ellen L.
    1984 "The Homelessness Problem." *Scientific American.* 251: 40-45.

    A general, yet stimulating discussion of the problem of homelessness in America. This article places special emphasis on how mental illness among many homeless people complicates their plight.

Bittner, Egon
    1967 "The Police on Skid Row: A Study in Peace-Keeping." *American Sociological Review.* 32: 699-715.

    This is one of the classic studies in the sociology of policing. The focus of Bittner's analysis is the "peace-keeping" function of the police that operates independently of and in the shadow of the law enforcement function. Bittner identifies several peace-keeping methods that are outcomes of officers' conceptions of the nature of social life among skid row residents.

Finn, Peter and Monique Sullivan

> 1988 *Police Response to Special Populations: Handling the Mentally Ill, Public Inebriate, and the Homeless.* Washington: U. S. Department of Justice, National Institute of Justice.

The authors develop the notion of social service "networks" that share the responsibility for dealing with "special populations." They provide a summary overview of features found in twelve communities in which networking has been attempted, and review some of the problems in organizing networks and the benefits to be derived from them.

Hanewicz, Wayne B., Lynn M. Fransway and Michael W. O'Neil

> 1982 "Improving the Linkages between Community Mental Health and the Police." *Journal of Police Science and Administration.* 10: 218-223.

The authors of this essay adopt the notion that police officers are the "gatekeepers" to other social service agencies. Although somewhat limited by a narrow focus on the link between the police and community health agencies, this paper provides a useful discussion of the problems encountered when police attempt to make referrals to alternative social service agencies.

Case Seventeen

Her First Job

PART ONE

Holly Martin loved her new job at Glendenning's Department Store. She turned 16 not long before taking the position, and even though it was part-time, she was very happy because it was her first job. The personnel manager at Glendenning's had assigned Holly to the fine china and glassware department. She would rather have been assigned to "Teen Fashions" or the music and record department, still, she was learning many new things every time that she came to work.

The best part of the job from Holly's viewpoint was that she was now no longer dependent on an allowance from her parents in order to have money to spend. Even though she was paid only a little more than minimum wage, she was relieved of the burden of having to ask her parents for money when she wanted to buy something, and even more important, she was now earning enough to buy neat clothes that really expanded her wardrobe. Many of the most attractive fashions she wanted were just too expensive for her allowance and Holly hated the idea of having to justify to her mom why she "needed" clothes, jewelry, and cosmetics that were "so expensive."

Holly was also able to expand her purchasing power when she shopped at Glendenning's. It was the policy of the store that employees could buy almost all items in the store at a 10% discount. Furthermore, if an employee applied for a Glendenning's credit card they were entitled to an even larger discount off the ticket price of merchandise. Since the company wanted to encourage use of the store's credit system, employees were given a 20% discount on merchandise if they charged the purchase to their credit account.

The rationale for this was twofold. First, like most other retailers, Glendenning's was able to profitably operate the system from the interest they received from credit accounts that carried forward a balance from one month to the next. Since the store was providing a service to its customers by permitting them to buy on credit and carry the balance forward, it was perfectly legitimate to charge a fee in the form of interest on unpaid balances. Secondly, corporate managers had known for a long time that their employees were some of their very best customers. Given the hundreds of employees who worked for the Glendenning Corporation, it was not surprising that a significant proportion of sales were to people who worked in the various Glendenning's outlets. Ultimately, the combination of store size and high quality, employee familiarity with the stores, convenience, and good discounts, were a powerful incentive for employees to shop at their workplace, and this they did in great numbers.

Sometimes the incentive to buy Glendenning's merchandise was so great that employees developed buying habits that came close to exceeding their abilities to pay for the items they had purchased. It was not unusual, for instance, for Glendenning's employees to carry fairly large credit balances over long periods of time. As long as employees—like other customers—paid the minimum monthly payment ($15.00) and stayed within their credit limit, the corporation would not quibble with customers regarding the magnitude of the existing balance. After her first month on the job, Holly Martin had accumulated charges on her credit card account that she, herself, realized would get to be a problem if she didn't slow down her rate of purchasing. Still, through the first month of her employment with Glendenning's, Holly very much enjoyed the opportunities and freedom of an independent consumer. All of this was made possible by her first job.

As she began her second month on the job, Holly was beginning to build a reputation as a good worker who was reliable and able to deal with customers in a polite and efficient manner. This was not always easy to do. Transactions over the counter of the fine china department often involved customers who had very exacting tastes in merchandise and were making very expensive purchases. In spite of her youth, Holly's supervisor was very pleased with both the quality of her interaction with these customers and her willingness to learn the details of the various lines of china and glassware that were included in Glendenning's inventory.

Also during her second month at work, Holly met LuRay and Dawn. Although the girls worked in different departments, they often met in the employee lounge since they typically took their breaks at the same time. Both LuRay and Dawn were a little older than Holly, and both had worked for Glendenning's for over a year. Because of their age and similar interests, Holly quickly learned to depend on LuRay and, especially, Dawn, for insight into the operations of a major department store.

On one occasion Holly confided to the other girls that she thought she was running up too many charges too quickly on her Glendenning's credit card. She was initially surprised and hurt that LuRay and Dawn only giggled as Holly described her problem to them.

"I suppose you just think I'm dumb?" Holly protested.

"Maybe dumb, maybe just uninformed," LuRay observed. "Dawn, you explain it to her. I've gotta go back to work."

"What's she talking about?" asked a confused Holly.

"Well, if you understood the system, you'd realize that only a nubbie would run up a big credit card balance at this place."

"But if you don't use your credit card, you lose half your discount," said Holly in bewilderment.

"That's not what I'm talking about, you silly goose. If you use your credit account right, you can get more than your discount."

"I don't understand what you mean. Quit teasing me," said Holly as her voice began to rise.

"Not so loud," invoked Dawn. "I'll explain what I mean if you promise to keep this little secret just between us."

"OK," Holly replied. "How many people who work here have store credit cards?" Dawn asked.

"Gee, everybody, I guess," Holly responded.

"You've got that right," instructed Dawn. "And don't you think that just about everybody uses theirs too?"

"I suppose."

"How close do you think the company watches those accounts?" asked Dawn. "I don't know," said Holly. "I guess they would cut you off if you charged too much. Then you'd have to pay off a bunch of the balance before they would let you use your credit card again."

"Maybe, but who cares about that?" smirked Dawn.

"Huh?" replied Holly.

"You know how to credit a charge card account for merchandise that is returned to the store, right?" Dawn asked.

"Yea," replied Holly. "So?"

"Well, what happens to that account?" Dawn inquired further.

"It gets a credit in the amount of the purchase, I guess."

"Brilliant!" observed Dawn. "Now, what would happen if you brought back stuff you had bought and gave yourself a credit?"

"You know we aren't allowed to do credit transactions on ourselves."

"Oh, yes, that's right," Dawn remarked with mock recollection. "But there wouldn't really be anything to stop you from doing a credit to your account if you put somebody else's I.D. number on the credit slip."

"You mean if I made it look like some other clerk rang up the transaction?" asked Holly.

"Yea, that really wouldn't be that hard to do."

"But wouldn't that be dishonest?" Holly inquired.

"Why? It's just a store rule, it's not against the law," Dawn responded.

"O.K., so what's the point?"

"It's like this," Dawn began. "There's really no reason for you to have much of a balance on your credit card at the end of the month. In fact, you could easily have a surplus of credits to your account! Every once in a while you should copy the inventory control number off some item on the floor and use somebody's I.D. number to write a sales return slip with a credit to your account. Presto! You've got $60 or $70 worth of shopping you can do in the future at no real cost."

"Are you kidding?" Holly replied. "You can't do that. That's stealing!"

Dawn replied with disdain. "No, it's not! Are you stealing money out of the cash register or something like that?"

"No, but . . ."

Dawn interrupted. "Is it shoplifting, grabbing stuff like some lowlife, then running out of the store?"

"But what if you get caught?" Holly rejoined.

"You simpleton, everybody does it. Do you see anybody getting caught? The whole trick is not to get carried away with it."

"I'm not sure I could do that," observed Holly. "I mean, I think I'd get caught if I tried to do it."

"Doing it is the best part of it," suggested Dawn. "It's incredibly easy to do. Just go about your business as you normally would. Run up a few credits now and then. When you're ready to go shopping you can browse all you want, and then when you see something you really want just charge it and they will subtract the cost of the item from the credits that you've built up. It's really easy and it's kind of fun too."

"I don't know," said Holly. "It sounds scary to me."

"Come on, give it a try," implored Dawn. "I bet you'll get into it after you've done it a couple of times."

PART TWO

In the three months that followed Holly's discussion with Dawn about the latter's approach to holding down the balance on a Glendenning's credit card account, Holly had used Dawn's suggestions a number of times. In time, Holly got accustomed to the practice and thought that more good than harm had come from her ringing up credits to herself.

Holly's problems began when Elenore Simpson talked to another employee about some strange behavior by Holly that she and the other person had both observed. Employee thefts, when they occurred, often involved clerks floating around in areas where they did not work. Merchandise would be removed from an area, carried back, and hidden in the departments where the employee-thief worked. Then the item or items would be removed from the store when the deviant employee left work at the end of his or her shift.

Mrs. Simpson and the other worker had seen elements of this in Holly's behavior. Holly had been observed passing through various departments where she was not assigned, handling merchandise, and apparently recording information listed on the items or on their price tags. While Holly did not appear to be stealing the items in question, her behavior was nevertheless suspicious.

Not wishing to confront Holly directly, Mrs. Simpson contacted the security manager of Glendenning's and told him about what she had seen. He too thought that the behavior was suspicious, but did not know exactly what to make of it. Realizing that no employee should be accused of dishonesty without real evidence, the security manager, Bill Howells, decided to place Holly Martin under camera surveillance and to have security personnel keep an eye on her. What they discovered was that Holly spent an inordinately large portion of *every* shift roaming the aisles outside the fine china department in a number of other areas of the store. While in these other areas, Holly would *always* remove items from the rack or shelf and record information from the price tag. On various occasions, she was observed—prior to the beginning of her shift, or at the end of one—actually purchasing these same items by checking out at the closest register and always using her credit card to "pay" for the item.

Bill Howells was familiar with how the scam described to Holly by Dawn operated. Careful employees who engaged in this practice were hard to catch. The security staff at Glendenning's simply did not have the time or the resources to scrutinize the thousands of transactions that involved employees as customers of the store. If employees became careless or overly bold in stealing merchandise or defrauding the store, there was usually a means of detecting their behavior. In this instance, Howells decided to examine a computer print-out of credit card transactions that was called a "return exception report." The report flagged the records of all credit card customers whose accounts consisted of a set of transactions in which 25% or more were alleged returns of merchandise. For any customer to return more than one in four of his/her purchases with a credit to an account was an extremely high rate of return. This was usually suggestive of potentially illegal transactions. Such information was used to initiate a more detailed examination of the history of transactions for any account.

The analysis of Holly Martin's credit card transactions yielded astonishing results. The record of her credit transactions with Glendenning's for the four months that she had worked at the store revealed that over $8,000 in credits had been posted to her account by way of merchandise that had supposedly been returned to the store. Amazingly, she had accumulated credits at a rate that greatly exceeded the $5,000 worth of purchases she had made during the three months she had been posting phony credits to her account. According to the record of the account, Glendenning's, in essence, owed Holly Martin $3,000!

When confronted with the evidence against her, Holly's basic defense was that she didn't really think she was stealing since "there was no money involved." When asked why she posted so many credits in so short a period of time, her only reply was that the procedures she needed to use were "easy" and that after a while, she really didn't think anymore about the chance that she might get caught. She pointed out that the approach she used permitted her to "buy" things she really needed and that she had gained a lot of popularity with her friends by being able to buy them lots of nice gifts.

Glendenning's terminated Holly's employment with the store and, because of her age, had a petition filed against her in juvenile court. Holly pleaded with the store manager not to fire her. She told the manager that she was basically an honest person and that she didn't want to be fired from her very first job—a job she really liked.

DISCUSSION QUESTIONS

1. Even in light of the evidence in this case, many people might resist the notion that Holly Martin and her friends, Luray and Dawn, are criminals. What do you think?
2. To what extent do you attribute Holly's behavior to her association with LuRay and Dawn? What is the likelihood that Holly would have defrauded Glendenning's if she had never met the other young women?
3. Does Glendenning's share any of the fault for Holly's behavior? Do you think that in some ways store policy presented incentives and opportunities to steal from the company?
4. How does Holly's misbehavior compare with that of an ordinary shoplifter? Should the company and police treat employee fraud and customer theft differently? Why or why not?
5. Should Holly and her friends be punished for what they have done? How should they be punished?

SUGGESTED READING
"HER FIRST JOB"

Altheide, David L., Patricia A. Adler, Peter Adler and Duane A. Altheide
1978 "The Social Meaning of Employee Theft." pp. 90-123 in J.M. Johnson and J.D. Douglas (eds.) *Crime at the Top*. Philadelphia: J.B. Lippincott.

The authors examine employee theft from an employee's viewpoint. They draw a number of conclusions that enhance our understanding of "Her First Job." Most striking perhaps is the finding that theft is typically embedded in a matrix of social symbols focused more on equity and self-worth than on greed.

Hollinger, Richard D. and John P. Clark
1982 "Employee Deviance: Response to the Perceived Quality of the Work Experience." *Work and Occupations*. 9: 97-114.

Job dissatisfaction has generally been considered a prime source of deviance in the workplace. Hollinger and Clark analyze the relationship between several deviant practices in the workplace and various measures of job satisfaction. While finding a degree of support consistent with the job satisfaction-workplace crime hypothesis, the authors conclude that an adequate explanation of occupational deviance must include other factors related to the total social context of the workplace.

Hollinger, Richard D. and John P. Clark
1982 "Formal and Informal Social Controls of Employee Deviance." *Sociological Quarterly*. 23: 333-343.

Holly Martin was introduced to the practice of employee fraud by fellow employees and initially detected by another store clerk. The strong influence of informal sanctions (from other employees) on occupational deviance is well-documented in this study. As predicted by the authors, their findings show that social control by co-workers has a greater salience for workplace behavior than does formal attempts by management to control employee deviance.

Hollinger, Richard D. and John P. Clark

1983   *Theft by Employees*. Lexington, MA: D.C. Heath.

This monograph consists of a comprehensive study of workplace theft. The authors explore a number of issues including the prevalence of theft in business organizations, the circumstances under which these crimes occur, and an assessment of the steps that managers can use to reduce the prevalence of employee theft.

Mars, Gerald

1982   *Cheats at Work: An Anthropology of Workplace Crime.* London: George Allen and Unevin.

This is an excellent qualitative study of a variety of types of occupational crime based primarily on British examples. The author presents a classification scheme for "fiddles" (as they are known in England) that cut across a number of occupational contexts. Also included in the study is a comparative analysis of the legal and extralegal or illegal rewards of the workplace.

Robin, Gerald D.

1974   "White-Collar Crime and Employee Theft." *Crime and Delinquency.* 20: 251-262.

Are employee thieves white-collar criminals? The intent of this article is to provide an answer to this question by exploring the conceptual relationship between white-collar crime, employee theft, and occupational crime. The author concludes that occupational crime is a larger conceptual category than either white-collar crime or employee theft, and that the latter two concepts should be treated as separate categories of criminality subsumed under the rubric of occupational deviance.

Zietz, Dorothy

1981   *Women Who Embezzle or Defraud: A Study of Convicted Felons.* New York: Praeger.

Zietz's study deals with the behavior of women convicted of property crimes, especially embezzlement and fraud. One goal of the book is to provide a gender-based comparison with the findings from Donald Cressey's classic study of men convicted of violations of financial trust. The case studies of a number of women who had committed fraud, and their rationales for doing so, are particularly interesting.

Case Eighteen

I Want My Property Returned

Middleton International Airport was busy as usual. So was Lowell Erlebacher, and he wondered why the rest of the world had so much difficulty understanding this fact. Lowell was quite perturbed by his situation; although he was home—he lived in Middleton—he was actually just passing through the airport on his way to Kansas City. Unfortunately his flight from Pittsburgh had been delayed on take-off causing him to miss his connecting flight. As he stood at the ticket counter trying to rearrange his schedule, he pondered the many petty hassles that plagued the lives of modern business executives.

Finally, after standing in line for fifteen minutes, Lowell was ready to travel again. Shock waves overcame him, however, as he reached downward for his briefcase. It was gone!

"Hellfire!" he exclaimed as he shot an evil eye first at the reservation clerk and then at the other travelers.

"Is something wrong?" asked the woman behind him.

"You could say that." Erlebacher rejoined menacingly. "I've just had a $200 briefcase walk away."

"Oh no," the woman sighed. "A young man, very nicely dressed, picked up a briefcase when he left the line just a few minutes ago. He was behind you and in front of me when I got in line."

"He looked anxious and in a hurry," the woman observed innocently. "I thought he was tired of standing in line. I'm so sorry."

Lowell Erlebacher was sorry too. How, he asked himself, could that air-headed woman let someone walk off with his brief case? No wonder the city was crime-ridden; people simply will not make the slightest effort to help one another.

Caught in the double bind of needing to catch a plane in twenty minutes *and* recognizing that without a police report he could not file an insurance claim, he cancelled his trip to Kansas City (he would be arriving late anyway). He hoped that tomorrow would bring him better luck.

Detective Karen Collins worked as an investigator with the Transit Authority Police. Her department was responsible for law enforcement within all transit authority facilities. She arrived at the ticket office of West-Central Airlines shortly after the theft had been reported. From the information provided by Mr. Erlebacher and other witnesses, it appeared that his victimization was similar to a series of other thefts that had occurred in and around the airport. The thief or thieves involved in these crimes had a definite preference for relatively lightweight, but expensive items.

Generally, they would exploit distracted travelers who appeared to be in an excessive hurry or impatient with the pace of things around the airport. Curbside taxi zones, restrooms, telephone stations, baggage claims areas—were all prime locations for this pattern of thefts. Mr. Erlebacher's loss was typical. He had been carrying a handsome leather briefcase that contained an expensive business calculator, a gold pen set, a compact tape recorder, and about $100 in cash. In total, the loss would amount to about $550 dollars, not including the business papers that were also stolen.

Theft investigations for Karen Collins usually began with a visit to several pawnshops that were scattered along the strip that led from downtown Middleton to the airport. The cooperation she received from pawnbrokers, as well as the brokers' reluctance to accept suspicious items, varied. The likelihood that she would recover stolen property from airport thefts, therefore, was highly dependent upon the cooperation of shopowners and the relative sophistication of the thief. Many brokers, realizing that they could be stuck with a loss if they accepted "hot items," simply refused to discuss their transactions with the police. Others would not accept pawned items unless the seller could provide positive identification. Many thieves actually saw this as no obstacle to stealing. Not surprisingly, the theft of items from airport travellers was highly attractive both in terms of the direct pay-off in stolen merchandise, and also in the low risk of apprehension. Many airport travelers never reported thefts to the police, while out-of-town victims would report thefts, accept recovered property, but were unwilling to assist in the prosecution of a theft suspect. Such assistance often implied a return to Middleton to testify against the suspect and this was something most victims would not do. In short, Detective Collins' ability to recover property was fairly good, but her ability to secure convictions was much more difficult.

Lowell Erlebacher was impressed by the good news. He had just returned from his delayed trip to Kansas City when Detective Collins showed up at the front door of his home with his tape recorder in hand. Collins had talked to a pawnshop owner who had accepted the recorder on the same afternoon of Erlebacher's victimization. Neither the shopkeeper nor the thief had played the "flip side" of the tape that was in the machine. The voice on the tape began, "Erlebacher-Weis Enterprises meeting with Sanderson Corporation, August 15, Pittsburgh, Pennsylvania. Lowell Erlebacher for Erlebacher-Weis; Walter Sanderson, Jim Cook, and Cathy McDonald for Sanderson."

"Outstanding!" Erlebacher exclaimed gleefully. "What about the other items?"

Detective Collins explained that the individual who had pawned the tape recorder used a driver's license to establish identification at the pawnshop. She drove to the address listed on the license and encountered the roommate of the person whom she believed had stolen the property. On a kitchen counter, clearly in view of the apartment door, Collins saw a briefcase that fit the description of the one stolen from Erlebacher. Collins questioned the roommate about the item. Seeking to avoid being implicated in the crime, the roommate was perfectly cooperative. He conceded that he had not seen the briefcase before and that he did not know where it had come from. He agreed that the initials "L.W.E." embossed under the handle were not his roommate's initials. The roommate willingly allowed Collins to examine the contents of the brief case and to look around the apartment. Although the calculator, pen set, and money Erlebacher claimed to have lost could not be located, the kitchen trash basket contained a number of papers with Erlebacher-Weis letterhead. Collins seized the briefcase as evidence and told the person in the apartment to tell the roommate that she would most surely be back for a return visit.

"Wonderful," Erlebacher reiterated.

"I think we ought to be able to get your other things back without too much trouble," observed Collins.

"Super! That's great!"

Karen Collins explained to Erlebacher that she had made an arrest in the case and that the evidence from her investigation had been turned over to the district attorney's office. She pointed out that he should expect a visit from a case investigator from the DA's office who would be responsible for preparing the case for prosecution. As she got up to leave, she noticed a troubled look on Erlebacher's face.

"Hang on a second, we're not through yet," he interjected with some chagrin. "I haven't got time to fool around with a court case. You've done a nice piece of policework here. You should be proud of what you have accomplished, but I'm a busy man and I think you ought to be able to wrap this thing up without me. I want my property returned. That's all. I do not want to be bothered with this anymore. Am I making myself clear?"

Having said his piece, Erlebacher was surprised by the angered and shocked look returned to him by Detective Collins and by the abruptness with which she headed for the door.

"Well, what the hell's the matter with her?" Erlebacher thought to himself. "Now she's looking at me like I'm the criminal. I thanked her for what she's done, what more does she want?"

On her drive back to the airport Karen Collins felt sick and on the verge of tears. She had departed Erlebacher's residence quickly and quietly in order to prevent herself from losing her temper. She understood quite well why airport travelers from Los Angeles would not return to Middleton to testify to the theft of a suitcase full of dirty laundry, but this case was different. This guy lived in town, there was a solid case against the thief, and little more than a single afternoon in court would be required for his testimony. In fact, the evidence against the thief and the knowledge that Erlebacher was on the witness list would probably be enough to cause the defense attorney to encourage his client to plead guilty. There was a good chance that Erlebacher would not need to testify at all.

The frustrations associated with her job were beginning to get to Collins. "I'm not a cop," she confided to herself. "I work for a collection agency."

She wondered if Erlebacher was aware of the dynamics of the courtroom workplace. "Does he know what the prosecutor's office is going to do when they discover that the victim is unwilling to testify against the suspect?" she thought. "This case is down the tubes if this guy doesn't cooperate."

Collins spun her car around and headed back toward Erlebacher's residence. This was more than she could tolerate. Too much effort had been sunk into this investigation to have it simply evaporate through noncooperation. Repressed anger was for the birds she thought. This victim was going to get a lecture in good citizenship. He may not realize it, but he was going to do his part even if she had to wheel him into the courthouse in a body cast.

As she neared Erlebacher's house she continued her conversation with herself. "Is this why the system was created? What about deterrence? Does this guy think that thievery is a onetime shot? What about retribution? No wonder the city is crime-ridden; people simply will not make the slightest effort to help one another."

Detective Collins murmured to herself as she approached the front door of the Erlebacher residence. "Brace yourself, jerk, an attitude adjustment is coming your way. No charge for home delivery."

DISCUSSION QUESTIONS

1. Considered as whole, how well did Detective Collins handle this case? What *grade* would you give Collins?
2. What are the elements of the crime in this case? What does it take to successfully perpetrate this type of offense? What would be the best policy for controlling theft in this kind of environment?
3. What factors explain Mr. Erlebacher's lack of interest in pursuing a conviction against the person who stole his brief case? Why did he bother to report the theft in the first place? Is he lazy, irresponsible, uninformed, or a careful manager of his own time?
4. Why does Detective Collins so firmly believe that the case against the thief will be lost without Erlebacher's cooperation? Is she exaggerating the importance of the victim's role in the prosecution of the crime?
5. Detective Collins appears to be very upset with Lowell Erlebacher's attitude toward the crime. Why? Is she justified in pursuing an angry confrontation with Erlebacher? Is this a prudent course of action?

SUGGESTED READING
"I WANT MY PROPERTY RETURNED"

Bureau of Justice Statistics

1989   *Criminal Victimization in the United States, 1987*. Washington: U.S. Department of Justice.

The Bureau of Justice Statistics reports findings from the National Crime Survey (NCS) on an annual basis. The 1987 report indicates that personal larceny is by far the most common form of victimization reported in the NCS. Interestingly, it is also one of the least reported; only 44% of personal larcenies (without contact) involving thefts of more than $50.00 are reported to police. Recovery of stolen property is the primary reason for not reporting thefts.

Cannavale, Frank J. and William D. Falcon

1976   *Witness Cooperation*. Lexington, MA: D.C. Heath.

This monograph reports the results of a major study conducted by the Institute for Law and Social Research into the problem of witness non-cooperation in criminal cases. The authors examine a wide range of witness attributes that are believed to influence an individual's willingness to cooperate in the prosecution of a case.

Cohen, Lawrence E., and David Cantor

1980   "The Determinants of Larceny: An Empirical and Theoretical Study." *Journal of Research in Crime and Delinquency*. 17: 140-159.

The authors provide an analysis of the social and demographic correlates of larceny victimization. The analysis is conducted from a "routine activities" perspective on criminal victimization. Findings from the research are interpreted in terms of the theory's major concepts of "motivated offenders," "suitable targets," and "absence of capable guardians".

Garofalo, James

1987   "Reassessing the Lifestyle Model of Criminal Victimization." pp. 23-42 in M.R. Gottfredson and T. Hirschi (eds.) *Positive Criminology*. Beverly Hills: Sage

Criminologists have known for sometime that the lifestyle that an individual leads affects the likelihood of becoming a victim of crime. In this article, Garofalo presents an overview of the lifestyle and "routine activities" approach to explaining crime victimization. His principle goal is to assess the original statement of the perspective in light of research findings that have accumulated in recent years.

Reiss, Albert

1974   "Discretionary Justice in the United States." *International Journal of Criminology and Penology*. 2: 181-205.

In this paper Reiss identifies three factors that influence a citizen's willingness to report a crime to the police. These include whether or not the property was insured, the victim's attitude toward the police, and the nature of the victim-offender relationship.

Case Nineteen

Don't Hurt My Mama

PART ONE

The early signs of spring were evident as the impatiens bloomed in the window boxes up and down 67th Avenue. Andy Jones and Chani ("Connie") Weaver, lifelong friends and playmates, sat on the front stoop outside Andy's mother's apartment. The two had been discussing the plight of Chani's mother when her son proposed a plan of action.

"You still got that piece you bought from Lerone?" Chani inquired.

"Yea, man, I got that thing squirreled away upstairs. So what?"

Chani paused to consider his response. "Well . . . I want to take it 'cause if that man starts whippin' up on Mama again, I aim to waste his ass!"

"Man, what's wrong with your head?" Andy rejoined as he jumped to his feet. Descending the two steps to street level, Andy turned and leaned forward to within six inches of Chani's nose to dramatize his point. "You get in Jo Jo's face with that gun, he's goin' to jerk it away from you and put in a place where the sun don't shine. Dig? What you talkin' about . . . skinny minnie like you? You ain't even goin' to phase him with no .22 pistol; you'd need a cannon to stop Jo Jo."

"We ll see 'bout that," retorted Chani. "You see what that dude did to Mama's face. Mama used to be a pretty lady. What if that punk did that shit to Daboo?"

Chani's remark caught Andy offguard. The woman called "Daboo" was, in fact, Andy's mother. In many ways she had been a surrogate parent to Chani as well. The man who had fathered Chani was married to Doretha Mangram, Andy's mother, at the time Chani was born. (Andy had been born to Mrs. Mangram during a marriage prior to her involvement with Chani's father.) From the day he was born, Doretha had held a special place in her heart for Chani. Onnie Weaver's life, it seemed, had been a series of foibles and misfortunes. To compensate for the care that Onnie found so difficult to give, Mrs. Mangram had brought Chani into her home from time to time to live with

131

her children and to care for him as well as her own modest circumstances would allow. As far back as Chani could remember, his nurturance and well-being had been a shared responsibility of his own mother and "Daboo."

The thought that a "boyfriend" would physically abuse his own mother had never occurred to Andy Jones. The comparison that Chani had drawn, unrealistic as it may have been, struck a cord with Andy. The "piece" that Chani had asked about was a "Saturday Night Special" that Andy had bought from his cousin several months earlier. The cousin, Lerone, had offered the weapon to Andy for $10. Given its affordability and the vague perception that it could provide a measure of self-protection under the right circumstances, Andy went ahead with its purchase. Although streetwise and tough, guns had never figured prominently in Andy's own survival strategies, thus, the weapon sat unused in the upstairs closet. Now, second thoughts caused Andy to override his fear that the gun would be turned on Chani and enkindled in him a deep loathing for the idea that Chani should stand by helplessly and watch his mother abused by her live-in boyfriend.

"Let's go get the piece," instructed Andy. "And, man, you make damn sure that you don't find your-genuine-individual-self eating the caps."

Chani shrugged, "It's cool, man. That jive turkey ain't never gonna know what hit him."

Chani's regard for his mother's safety was based on years of abuse that he had seen inflicted on her by a part-time boyfriend named Jo Jo Shivers. The relationship had begun six years earlier when Chani was only twelve years old. Initially, the relationship consisted of drinking, partying, and occasional sexual liaisons. Money in the Weaver household was always tight as Onnie Weaver had never held a full time job. In time Onnie realized that Shivers, who was also unemployed, had latched onto her primarily because her welfare checks provided him with a steady source of drinking money. Six months into the affair, Onnie tried to break off her relationship with Jo Jo; that was when the beatings began. From that point, Onnie suffered through Shivers' presence as best she could, fearful that the beatings would get even worse if she tried to rid herself of Jo Jo once and for all.

Onnie learned eventually that she had underestimated Shivers' brutality. Jo Jo had a community wide reputation as a bully, parasite, and mean-spirited drunk. Especially when he was drinking, which was most the time that he was around Onnie, Shivers displayed an unpredictable and violent temper. He followed a fairly stable pattern of living with the Weavers when it suited him; the rest of the time he stayed at his mother's apartment. Onnie discovered that when Jo Jo was around it made little difference whether she tried to appease him, avoid him, or simply go about her own business. The beatings grew progressively worse; it was clear that she had become the principal target of Shivers' foul disposition.

Chani Weaver was not exaggerating the magnitude of the injuries Onnie had received when he suggested to Andy Jones that she had been disfigured by Shivers' beatings. In the years that she had been seeing him, Onnie had been burned, stabbed, had bones broken by Shivers, and had been sexually assaulted. Onnie was twice hospitalized from being assaulted by Shivers.

Three years earlier, she spent five days in the hospital from injuries she had sustained from a beating administered by her drunken boyfriend. While drinking with

Onnie on her front porch, Shivers became enraged and began punching her face and head. As she rose from a lawn chair to try to escape his blows, Shivers punched her with sufficient force to knock her over the porch rail. She landed, unconscious, on the concrete steps five feet below the porch. The emergency room examination revealed that Onnie had sustained a broken nose, fractured cheekbones on each side of her face, two broken ribs, and multiple contusions. As a consequence of the blow to her ribs, a portion of Onnie's left lung filled with fluid, and the plural cavity between the lung and ribs became engorged with blood.

The medical social worker at the hospital contacted police investigators who, on the basis of the hospital examination, obtained a warrant charging Shivers with aggravated assault. The case was dismissed at the preliminary hearing after Onnie told an investigator from the district attorney's office that she would not testify against Jo Jo if the case came to trial. About eight months later, Shivers was arrested for another assault on Onnie and this time charged with simple battery. Again, Onnie refused to cooperate in the prosecution of the case.

PART TWO

Memorial Day began in the city with every indication that it was going to be hot. Stirred by the heat, Chani had gotten up early to have a bowl of cereal, watch morning cartoons, and formulate his plans to spend the afternoon with Andy Jones. Onnie Weaver was still sleeping at 10:30 when Jo Jo Shivers arrived carrying the remnants of a 12-pack of malt liquor. Perceiving no need to announce his arrival nor to request permission to enter the apartment, Jo Jo flung open the screen door and entered the kitchen. Shivers deposited the cardboard box of cans in the sink. Opening one as he turned around, Jo Jo encountered Chani who had left the living room to greet the morning intruder.

"Where's your mama, boy?" Shivers inquired bluntly.

Exasperated but yet cowed by Shivers early morning orneriness, Chani protested weakly, "She's still in bed. Why you got to come over here so early?"

"Watch your mouth, shortcake," Shivers retorted. "Why don't you go play?"

Shivers turned away from Chani and headed toward Onnie's bedroom. "Hey Squeeze!" Shivers bellowed as he stood in the doorway of Onnie's bedroom. What you be doin' sleepin' all day? Drag yo' ass outta' there, I want some company."

Bleary-eyed but expressionless, Onnie slowly rose to a sitting position at the side of the bed. She retrieved a sundress from a chair by the bed and pulled it over her head. Leaving the room she walked past Jo Jo who was still standing by the door. Her acknowledgement of Shivers presence was minimal. "Mornin," she murmured as she walked past him down the short hallway. "I gotta pee."

Moments later Onnie emerged from the bathroom still wiping the sleep from her eyes. Not yet ready to fully accept Jo Jo's presence, Onnie again strolled past him to position herself in front of the screen door. Staring across the alley, she observed to herself, "Goin' be hot, baby."

Now ready to acknowledge Jo Jo, she turned to him, fixing her eyes on his can of malt liquor. "How about a sip?" she inquired.

Without speaking, Shivers pointed to the sink. "They cold?" Onnie asked only half expecting Jo Jo to answer. Onnie pulled a can from the carton, opened it, and sat down at the kitchen table across from Shivers.

Jo Jo and Onnie took a little over an hour to finish what remained of the malt liquor. Chani had used the time to pull himself together in anticipation of going to Daboo's to find Andy. Aside from the abrasive but low key banter coming from the kitchen, the household was pretty quiet.

Suddenly, as had happened on too many occasions, the calm was broken by Shivers bellowing insult and innuendo at Onnie. This time the bone of contention was the liquor supply.

"What you mean, bitch? Don't you sit there on your fat ass, drink my brew, then tell me you ain't got no bread. If I knock your fuckin' shit loose, bet you'd find some cash."

Chani rushed to the kitchen to intervene. "Don't you hurt my Mama," said Chani in a tone mixed with anger and fear.

Shivers glared at Chani, knocking a chair to the floor as he rose. Onnie broke in, knowing that Shivers could easily have his way with the diminutive Chani. "Honey, go get my purse for me and don't argue," she instructed Chani.

Returning with the purse, Chani entered the kitchen. In one motion Shivers ripped the purse from the boy's hands, slinging it in the direction of Onnie. "Don't got no money?" Shivers invoked mockingly. "At the store, you best come across or I be puttin' you in a hurtin' way." Having said this, Shivers lunged at Onnie grabbing a fistful of hair as he dragged her, head first, toward the door. Onnie stumbled off the porch and down the back steps with Shivers not far behind. Chani followed helplessly and watched Jo Jo shove and kick Onnie as she stumbled down the alley. "Don't you hurt my Mama," Chani implored as Onnie and Jo Jo disappeared around the corner of the building headed in the direction of the liquor store two blocks away.

It took no more than twenty minutes for Onnie and Jo Jo to come back into view from the vantage point of Chani's front window. Onnie hugged what appeared to be another 12-pack of malt liquor in one arm and her purse in the other. Jo Jo continued to shove and swat at Onnie as they walked. Upon their return, Onnie dropped the 12-pack on the kitchen table and collapsed exhausted on a high-backed wooden chair.

Jo Jo was unrelenting in his abusiveness. Again, grabbing Onnie's hair, he pulled her head painfully backward as he stood over her shrieking obscenities and threats. Out of the corner of his eye he finally noticed Chani standing in the interior doorway of the kitchen with a .22 pistol pointed in his direction. Quickly, Jo Jo shifted completely behind Onnie and slipped his free arm under her chin. Using the back of the chair for leverage Shivers lifted Onnie by the throat over the back of the chair. "You want me to break this bitch's fuckin' neck?" taunted Shivers.

"I told you not to hurt Mama," Chani replied unflinchingly. "You're about to die, Mister."

Outraged by the thought that a mere boy would threaten him, Shivers loosened his distracted grip on Onnie's throat. Onnie began to sink back into her chair as Shivers scowled at Chani and took a half step in his direction. "So you be some kinda bad dude, huh? I'm goin' mop the flo' with . . ."

To Shivers' surprise, the gun discharged three times before he could finish his sentence. Each shot took effect: first, in Shiver's left arm just above the elbow, then in his left shoulder, the third shot ripped along the side of Shiver's face mangling his outer ear. Shivers stood bolt upright in disbelief. Before he could reorient himself, Shivers was twice again shot. The deep chest wounds turned his knees to jelly and Shivers fell to the floor breaking his fall with his one good arm. Chani's mother dashed for the back porch, screaming as she flew outside. Chani retreated down the hallway to his room to reload the gun.

Returning to the kitchen, Chani encountered Jo Jo Shivers standing about two feet from the back door with his back to the screen. Shivers staggered, a half step backward, a full step forward, Chani fired, again hitting Shivers in the chest. The wounded man slowly rotated toward the door and reached for the screen door. Chani shot once more causing Shivers to lurch outward. With his toes catching on the threshold of the back door, Shivers crashed to the floor of the porch. There he lay motionless and mortally wounded. He was dead by the time the police arrived.

PART THREE

"I don't care if he is dead," Chani Weaver had told an arresting officer. "I'd kill him again if he be doin' my mama that way!"

As he sat in his office in the public defender's office, Kevin Grey weighed two competing interpretations of what had happened on Memorial Day at the home of Onnie Weaver. Since Chani Weaver had been charged with murder in the death of Jo Jo Shivers, the interpretation of what had happened at the Weaver residence would have a tremendous impact on Chani Weaver's well-being.

On the one hand, it was undenied by all that Chani had borrowed the gun used to kill Shivers prior to the incident, with the intention of using it against Shivers. Wasn't this evidence of "malice aforethought," indicating that Chani had deliberately set out to do in Jo Jo? Further, Shivers had been shot seven times and Chani had actually taken time to reload the weapon during the course of the altercation. How could this be construed as self-defense? Lastly, Chani had shown no real remorse over the killing. How would this be factored in with the other evidence against him?

On the other hand, the record clearly showed that the Weavers had suffered from years of abuse from Shivers, a man with a reputation in the community for bellicose and brutish behavior. The medical records of Onnie Weaver were testimony to the fact that not only had she been the victim of severe injuries inflicted by Shivers, but that the abuse had gone on for a long time. Then there was a dual issue of self-defense. For an 18-year-old, Chani was exactly as Andy Jones had described him, a "skinny minnie." Chani was 5' 2" and weighed about 115 pounds. When Grey had visited Chani at the county jail shortly after his arrest, the boy was wearing a faded Hawaiian shirt, "jams", and shower clogs; physically, he looked like a twelve-year-old. Shivers was almost larger than *both* Weavers combined, mother and child. He stood over 6 ft. tall and weighed in excess of 200 pounds. Clearly, Chani Weaver would have been powerless to control Shivers through shear physical prowess. What about the actual incident? There was Chani's claim, substantiated by Onnie, that Jo Jo had threatened to break Onnie's neck and had actually had her in a position where he could have followed through on his threat. Given the escalating cycle of violence that had been directed against Onnie, a reasonable person might very well have believed that the threat to Onnie was substantial and real.

Kevin Grey decided that the best way to handle the potential conflict of interpretation in this case was to attempt to nip it in the bud; he would work toward having the case dismissed at the preliminary hearing on the grounds that the killing was a justifiable act in defense of Onnie Weaver. Since Magistrate John Walker was the consumate politician, it was unlikely in light of the grisly nature of the shooting that he would be inclined to dismiss the case. He would do so, however, if he sensed that the district attorney's office was not interested in prosecuting the case and would be willing to take the heat for any negative reaction that might accrue from a dismissal. Grey realized, therefore, that he would need to weaken the district attorney's motivation to prosecute the case. The best way to accomplish this was to share Onnie Weaver's medical record with the district attorney and to show the legacy of injury and abuse that Weaver had sustained at the hands of Jo Jo Shivers. His case was aided by the fact that the assistant district attorney who was handling the Chani Weaver case was an earthy, gun-toting, "tough guy" with a proven record of sympathy for people who used "self-help" methods to repel interpersonal aggression. (Not long after the hearing, the DA told Kevin Grey that he would have defended his mother in much the same way Chani had. The DA confided, however, that he would have done so sooner.)

On the day of the hearing, both the assistant DA and the investigator for the district attorney's office agreed that the case was unworthy of prosecution and that they were convinced that the killing was justifiable. This combined with Chani Weaver's pitiful appearance in court removed any reluctance on Judge Walker's part to dismiss the case.

Confronted by reporters as they left the courtroom, Kevin Grey was asked to explain the outcome of the case. "The true victims in this case are the family," he responded. "Their victimizer is deceased."

DISCUSSION QUESTIONS

1. What are the situational factors that predisposed Chani Weaver to kill Jo Jo Shivers? If you had been a neighbor of the Weaver's would you have been surprised by the killing?
2. Was Onnie Weaver partially to blame for her own plight? Why didn't she simply refuse to see or speak to Shivers?
3. What is the likelihood that Shivers would have eventually murdered Onnie Weaver? What factors might have constrained Shivers from killing her?

4. Should Chani Weaver have been tried for murder? What evidence from this case would you apply to this question?
5. Did the judge and the district attorney take a principled stand in the Weaver case? Were they convinced that the killing of Shivers met the legal requirements of justifiable homicide?

SUGGESTED READING
"DON'T HURT MY MAMA"

Black, Donald
    1983   "Crime and Social Control. *American Sociological Review*. 48: 34-45.

    This article develops the ironic notion that certain types of behavior share properties of both crime and social control. Although the state has monopolized much of the right to engage in violent social control, historically, modes of social control relied heavily on strategies of "self-help". Black argues, and the actions of Chani Weaver show, that self-help mechanisms of control are not as archaic as is sometimes thought.

Kantor, Glenda Kaufman and Murray A. Straus
    1987   "The 'Drunken Bum' Theory of Wife Beating." *Social Problems*. 34: 213-230.

    The authors examine the hypothesis that wife-beating is a result of violent inhibitions dulled by heavy alcohol use. The authors find that high rates of drinking are associated with assaults on wives but that acceptance of violence as appropriate conduct is a more important factor.

Kleck, Gary
    1988   "Crime Control Through the Private Use of Armed Force." *Social Problems*. 35 : 1-21.

    Kleck argues that armed defensive actions against violent victimization are about as common as legal mechanisms such as arrest. The article provides an overview of current knowledge regarding armed resistance to violent crime. Significantly, the evidence suggests that armed resistance has an impact on the prevention of injury from criminal assault that is greater than any other victim response to crime.

Luckenbill, David
    1977   "Criminal Homicide as a Situated Transaction." *Social Problems*. 25: 176-186.

    Luckenbill describes the social context of the many homicides that occur among acquaintances, friends, and relatives. Characterized as situated transactions, homicides often follow an escalating cycle of resentment that terminates in the death of one or more of the interactants. The article provides a particularly good analysis of the interactional nature of many forms of lethal violence.

McLeod, Maureen
    1988   "Victim Noncooperation in the Prosecution of Domestic Assault." *Criminology*. 21: 395-416.

    There is a relatively large research literature regarding the unwillingness of the police and prosecutors to process some types of criminal cases. The dynamics of victim noncooperation, on the other hand, are not well know though such noncooperation is fairly common in domestic assault cases. McLeod's article analyzes the willingness of domestic assault victims to cooperate with criminal justice personnel at several different decision-points in the criminal process.

Case Twenty

Honest John

PART ONE

It was time to pay bills at the Franklin household. Never a pleasant task, John Franklin was particularly chagrined by $822 in charges from the Worldwide Travel Club. Although he often travelled out-of-town on business, John knew that he had not charged trips to Las Vegas and Seattle to his travel club credit card; he had not even been to Seattle in May, and he had never been to Las Vegas in his life (and had no interest in going). The travel club had obviously screwed up. But getting unwarranted charges removed from his bill was probably going to be a pain in the neck. John decided that rather than put off calling Worldwide Travel he should contact them immediately so that they could correct the error on his bill and credit him for the overcharges.

John received quite a surprise when he contacted Worldwide Travel. "I'm sorry, Mr. Franklin," the billing agent responded. "Our records show that Mrs. Franklin charged an airline ticket to Las Vegas in the amount of $367 to your account on May 2, and a $455 first-class ticket to Seattle was charged to your account on May 15. Both of these were round-trip tickets."

Franklin failed to understand how this could be. He did not routinely keep track of his wife's comings and goings, but Las Vegas? Seattle, first class? Impossible!

"Are you sure this is the same Mrs. Franklin that I'm married to," he inquired.

"Sir, we would have no way of knowing that," she responded in the flat, nasal intonation of a reservationist. "I can tell you, however, that the tickets were definitely ordered with your account number and I do have two purchase orders that were signed by a 'Mrs. John Franklin.' "

John paused before he replied. "How can this be?" he asked.

"I don't know Mr. Franklin," the clerk answered with mock patience. "If you would like to come into the office, I would be glad to let you examine the purchase orders. Or maybe you would like to ask Mrs. Franklin about these charges before you come in?"

For reasons that were not even clear to himself, Franklin did not want to discuss this matter with his wife, Lynn, without having a better handle on what was going on here.

"How about if I stop in the first thing tomorrow morning?" he inquired.

"That would be fine, sir. I'm sorry that this has created a problem; hopefully we'll get things straightened out in the morning. My name is Jane, just ask for me when you arrive. Have a nice day, Mr. Franklin."

As Franklin sat down with the travel agent he was still puzzled about how these trips came to be charged to his credit card. His wife did have a travel club credit card of her own, it had the same account number as his card, but it was in his wife's name. As he examined the purchase orders, two things were clear—they were both signed by "Mrs. John Franklin," and they both carried an imprint of Franklin's card.

"Something's wrong here!" Franklin exclaimed as he reached for his wallet.

Largely for business reasons, John Franklin was the type of person who carried a large and diverse collection of credit cards. As he sorted through his set of more than thirty cards it was becoming clear to him that his Worldwide Travel Club card was missing. Franklin asked himself rhetorically how anyone could have stolen just one of his cards without stealing his whole wallet. He must have lost the card and never realized that it was missing.

"Well, I'll tell you what's going on here, Jane," he remarked to the travel agent. "It's pretty certain that somehow I misplaced my credit card, someone else found it, and now they are making fraudulent use of it. I certainly don't want anymore charges billed to this account and I suppose that you will want to have this person arrested because I am not going to pay for credit charges that I didn't authorize."

Jane Miller, the travel agent, excused herself so that she could find the agency manager and ask her to join the discussion. After spending a few minutes to familiarize herself with Franklin's account, the manager sat down next to John Franklin at the agent's desk.

"I'm sorry for what seems to have happened with your account, Mr. Franklin, but I need to explain a couple of things to you before anything can be done about your account." The manager continued, "I'm pretty sure that we can catch the person who has been misusing your card. With your cooperation, we will certainly have her arrested and charged for unauthorized use of one of our credit cards. In the meantime, we can prohibit any additional charges to your old account and we can issue you a new card with a new account number. But since you did not report your card as stolen, and charges have been made to your account, you are still legally responsible for $822 on the present account. For us to do anything about that, we will need a signed acknowledgment from you that the use of your credit card account was unauthorized and that you are willing to testify in court against the person who has misused your credit card."

"No problem," Franklin responded. "Where do I sign?"

"Well it's not that simple. We have had some very bad experience being caught in between estranged lovers, disgruntled business associates, and the like, over what constitutes 'unauthorized' use of one of our cards. In cases such as this, Worldwide

Travel will not waste the time of the police and DA's office, or risk being sued, if we do not feel that arrest and prosecution is justified and that a conviction is likely to be obtained. When we catch the culprit, we will ask you to come in and make a positive identification of the person and sign a statement that the person in question is not authorized to use your card. Then, we will have this individual arrested."

"But what if you don't catch her," Franklin inquired.

"Well, it's interesting that you should ask that. The person who has apparently been making fraudulent use of your card has made reservations for a trip to Cancun, Mexico. She intends to charge the tickets to your account and 'Mrs. Franklin' will come in and pickup the tickets later this week. I don't think she'll cancel out since she took a special fare; I expect we'll see her on Thursday."

"OK," Franklin responded. "I'll be in town on Thursday. Give me a call and I'll try to come on over and we'll get this mess straightened up."

By Thursday afternoon, John Franklin's cognizance of an impending phone call from Worldwide Travel was subsumed by the many preoccupations of office work. Finally, at 3:15 p.m. the phone rang.

"Mr. Franklin, this is Betty Scott, I'm the manager at Worldwide Travel. How are you this afternoon?"

"Fine," Franklin replied. "Do you have any news for me?"

"Yes, I do." said the manager. "We have a woman here who came by to pickup the ticket to Cancun. She will not give us her name, but she claims that you have given her permission to make purchases on your card under Mrs. Franklin's name."

"She said what?"

"That's what she said, Mr. Franklin. I'm sure that if you come over as soon as possible this can be cleared up right away."

Reaching for his sport coat as he hung up, Franklin responded, "Be there in about twenty minutes."

"Cancun?" Franklin asked himself during his drive to the Worldwide office. "My thief has some fairly exotic tastes." He also thought to himself that this particular crook must be bolder than brass. Had he been caught in this situation he was sure that he would have bolted for the door and been gone. "How is she going to convince these people that she's Lynn, with me present."

Not long after he arrived at Worldwide Travel John Franklin received his answer to this question. As he entered the office where the suspect was being held, he encountered an impeccably groomed young woman wearing a stylishly tailored business suit. A look of shocked disbelief etched its way across Franklin's face.

The young woman was the first to speak. "Ooh-ooh-ooh!" she exclaimed with staged exhilaration. "Well, if it isn't Honest John Franklin, him...self! Here's Johnny!"

Franklin stood speechless.

"What's the matter, John-John?" the woman inquired in babytalk. "The cat got your tongue? Has Johnny got a little problem? Been a bad boy? Yes! Yes! Yes!"

Betty Scott could make no sense of the situation. She could discern neither the source of the young woman's acerbic remarks to Franklin nor his speechlessness. Without taking sides, it was clear to her that the young woman was correct—something was bothering Franklin. What was his problem, anyway?

PART TWO

A few seconds that seemed like an hour had elapsed when John Franklin, without saying a word, motioned to Betty Scott to join him as he stepped out of the room. Once out of the room, they moved across the hall and into the manager's office. It was there that Franklin finally spoke up.

"Well, it's true," Franklin observed. "She has really created a problem for me this time. This woman's name is Lorraine Davis. In the past she has done work for me part-time. I have no need for her services anymore, but I'm afraid on the basis of her past performance and, now this incident, that she could create an incident that would really harm my business. Indeed, I did not authorize her to use my credit card and I'm not sure how she got a hold of it, but it's definitely not in my interest to get the police involved in this if we can avoid doing so."

"Personally, I think she should be punished," Betty Scott replied. "But as I said before, we are not going to have this case prosecuted without your cooperation. Are you telling me that you are authorizing her to use your card?"

"Oh no, not at all," Franklin exclaimed. "Isn't there some way short of calling the police that we can get her to pay the bill for this."

"Mr. Franklin, let me remind you that as it stands now we have no legal claim against Ms. Davis. Unless you are willing to acknowledge that the charges on the credit card were not authorized by you, the debt remains yours, Mr. Franklin, not Ms. Davis'."

"But now that we know who's been doing this, can't you close the account and just write off the bogus charges? Surely, you have insurance to cover this sort of thing?"

"Get serious, Mr. Franklin," Betty Scott retorted. "I told you earlier that we can cancel the ticket to Cancun, though that may cost us because the ticket was part of a special offer. Even if we cancel the present reservation, there's the matter of the $822 in previous charges. If we can show credit card fraud, then we can recoup our loses through insurance; otherwise, that debt belongs to you, Mr. Franklin."

Pursing his lips as he stared into space, Franklin remarked, "This situation stinks!"

"Perhaps so," Ms. Scott rejoined. "But I can't hold that woman here all day. We need to reach a decision about what we are going to do. We can call the police and take your statement, or you can start thinking about paying the existing charges on your account. How's it going to be, Mr. Franklin?"

PART THREE

Across the hall in the other office, Lorraine Davis sat under the watchful eye of Jane Miller. Unruffled, but bored by the silence, Davis began to tell her side of the story at the same time that John Franklin was attempting to negotiate with Betty Scott. Jane listen intently at first and later with bemusement.

"John Franklin," Davis began, "is a little bitty boy parading around in a big man's body. Do you folks have to rely on cooperation from him before you can call the police?"

"Yes, I think so," Jane replied.

"Well then, I'm home free," Davis responded confidently. "Don't expect much from him."

"Why not?" Jane inquired.

"Let's see," Davis replied, "my guess is that right now, John is over there trying to beg your manager not to call the police. In his heart he's feeling sorry for himself, like he's some big-time victim of crime. In his head, he knows he's as much of a deviate as I'll ever be."

"I don't have any idea what you're talking about," Miller said.

"Let me make myself clear to you then," directed Davis. "He is in no position to tell you how I got a hold of his credit card, so he's probably trying to arrange some way to get the travel agency to absorb the loss or otherwise get you to come after me."

Jane interrupted, "I don't think we can do that."

"Right," Davis rejoined. "So why doesn't he cooperate with you and have you call the police? Why do you suppose he acted like such a dummy when he first saw that I was 'Mrs. Franklin.'"

"I don't know." said Jane. "Your relationship with him is a real mystery to me."

"Well, you might say that I've worked for him from time to time," Davis said wryly.

"It's none of my concern," Miller confessed, "but are you and he into crooked business dealings?"

"No, not at all," Davis confided. "You see, some of that little boy in Johnny causes him to want to spend big bucks on, well, 'professional girl friends,'" Davis smiled knowingly, awaiting a response from Jane.

"I still don't get it," Jane sighed.

Lorraine Davis leaned forward in her chair. "I'm a professional call girl," whispered Davis. "You know—a high-priced whore."

"Oh, my God!" Miller shrieked. "I can't believe it!"

"Fooled you, didn't I," Davis grinned.

Jane Miller's mood changed from shock and disbelief to an appreciation of the semi-comic nature of the situation. "May I assume that when you took his credit card you sort of caught him with his pants down?"

"I performed the full range of services and the bastard never, ever left a tip," observed Davis. "I figured he owed me."

"I can see why he doesn't want to call the police," Jane noted.

"Oh yea!" remarked Davis. "If his lovely wife finds about his 'travels,' Mr. Honest John will probably have a 2x4 laid atop his wimpy head. I suspect he will be writing you a check real soon."

As Lorraine Davis and Jane Miller concluded their conversation, John Franklin was across the hall with pen in hand.

"Do you mind if I cover this in two payments?" he inquired.

"Not at all, Mr. Franklin," Betty Scott responded. "Is there any need for us to detain Ms. Davis?"

"I guess not," Franklin replied.

As they entered the hallway of the travel agency, Scott again expressed apologies for the trouble caused Franklin.

"Expensive date," Franklin muttered in response as he headed toward the door.

"Excuse me?" Scott asked.

"Never mind," shrugged Franklin as he continued down the hall. "Just talking to myself."

"OK" Scott rejoined with practiced enthusiasm, "You have a nice day, Mr. Franklin. Bye-Bye!"

DISCUSSION QUESTIONS

1. John Franklin is in a "double-bind." Can you describe his problem? What are the countervailing social forces that have undermined his interest in seeing that Lorraine Davis is prosecuted?
2. Prostitution is commonly considered a victimless crime, yet most people would concede that there are indirect costs that can accrue from this type of deviance. Is the "Honest John" case an example of this?
3. To what extent, if any, did John Franklin participate in his own victimization? What are some other examples of situations that involve victim-precipitated crime?
4. What is the basis for the travel agency's refusal to file a complaint without Franklin's cooperation? What would happen if they pressed charges anyway?
5. How does this case illustrate the obstacles to full enforcement of the law? Was the outcome of this series of events "just?"

SUGGESTED READING
"HONEST JOHN"

Geis, Gilbert
> 1979   *Not the Law's Business*. New York: Schocken
>> This monograph provides a comprehensive overview of a number of behaviors that are commonly subsumed under the rubric "victimless crime". Chapter Five of the book is an in-depth discussion of both the behavioral and legal dimensions of prostitution.

Hall, Donald
> 1975   "The Role of the Victim in the Prosecution and Disposition of a Criminal Case." *Vanderbilt Law Review*. 28: 932-985.
>> Hall identifies the many junctures at which victims are called upon to assist in the prosecution of criminal cases. The author discusses the highly relevant issue of victim-police interaction in case processing. The claim that the police are less likely to prosecute cases that involve suspect behavior by the crime victim is especially noteworthy.

Harold Holtzman and Sharon Pines

1982   "Buying Sex: The Phenomenology of Being a John." *Deviant Behavior*. 4: 89-116.

This article reports findings from interviews with individuals who had purchased the services of prostitutes. The authors discover that there are four phases involved in the pursuit of commercial sex. Of particular interest to the case, "Honest John," is the last phase that deals with the aftermath of encounters with prostitutes.

MacNamara, Donal and Edward Sagarin

1977   *Sex, Crime, and the Law*. New York: The Free Press.

As the title suggests, this book examines the relationship between a variety of "sex crimes" and the law. The authors in their chapter on prostitution discuss "prostitution and concomitant crime." One subcategory under this heading involves crimes by prostitutes against their customers.

Winick, Charles

1962   "Prostitutes' Clients' Perceptions of the Prostitutes and of Themselves." *International Journal of Social Psychiatry*. 8: 289-297.

This is an interesting study of the attributions that clients of prostitutes make about the behavior of prostitutes and their own behavior. Aside from drug addiction and the prospect of contracting a sexually transmitted disease, the majority of respondents reported no negative attributions about prostitute behavior.